BEAD POWER

A Magical Journey into the World of Beads

CAROLYN MANZI

To Alyssa:
May your creativity take you on many magical Adventures!
Bead on!
Carolyn ☆

THREE RIVERS PRESS • NEW YORK

Published by Three Rivers Press, New York, New York. Member of the Crown Publishing Group.

Random House, Inc. New York, Toronto, London, Sydney, Auckland
www.randomhouse.com

THREE RIVERS PRESS is a registered trademark and the Three Rivers Press colophon is a trademark of Random House, Inc.

Printed in the United States of America

Technical Illustrator: Joseph Leone

Library of Congress Cataloging-in-Publication Data

Manzi, Carolyn.
    Bead power : a magical journey into the world of beads / Carolyn Manzi.—1st ed. (pbk.)
    1. Beadwork. 2. Beads—Folklore. 3. Beads—Religious aspects. I. Title.
TT860.M33 2001
745.58'2—dc21   2001027351

ISBN 0-609-80873-7

10 9 8 7 6 5 4 3 2 1

First Edition

This book is dedicated to my mother,
Carol Madsen Manzi, and
to the memory of my grandmother,
Lucia Manzi (1882-1967),
with great love and thanks for
all they taught me.

The true voyage of self-discovery lies in not seeking new landscapes but in having new eyes.

—Marcel Proust

CONTENTS

INTRODUCTION

For as long as I can remember, I have lived under the spell of beads. When I was a small child, my Italian grandmother and my aunt introduced me to the Catholic rosary. I spent endless hours of my childhood making rings, bracelets, and chokers out of seed beads, wire, and broken crystal necklaces. By third grade, beads adorned the fringe on my purse, the fringe on my bike handlebars, and my stuffed animals' outfits. I felt a certain power and joy in embellishing my body and my world in just the right way.

As an adult, I was reintroduced to beads by my friend Susan Pacitto. My love for beads was reawakened the first time I walked into her bead shop on Cape Cod. When I opened the door to her magical world of Austrian crystals, African trade beads, Tibetan prayer boxes, wampum, and other treasures, I felt like I was coming home.

Since then my love for beads has grown stronger and taken me on many fascinating adventures into the worlds of culture, color, and bead magic. There is a force that bonds humans to beads and sets one off in pursuit of the other. In this ancient dance of attraction, I have often wondered, who is the pursuer and who is the pursued? Writing this book has finally allowed me to answer this question.

Bead Power explores personal and global bead history and presents beads in the context of creating art, healing, rituals, relationships, and change in our lives. I invite you to join me on this journey of "intentional beading." For those unfamiliar with the concept, creating art with intention means focusing our vision on that which we wish to create in our lives, and then making power objects to help manifest our vision in physical reality.

I also explore the concept of the bead as a powerful symbol for invoking healing in our lives. Symbols work on a deep unconscious level to transform our vision and the way we experience the world. Symbolic vision is inclusive, relationship oriented, and intuitive. Beads are a symbol for wholeness and connection. Beads are a symbol for multiculturalism and diversity in our world.

Although we live in technologically advanced times, we still have a long way to go in our evolution toward becoming tolerant, loving, and accepting. Learning about beads teaches us to respect, appreciate, and revere the beauty and diversity of our multicultural world. Incorporating elements of global culture into our lives enriches our experience and bonds us to one another. Beads, for many diverse cultures throughout history, have been the symbol that inspires connection with spiritual power.

At the end of this book, there is a section of
illustrations that includes a bead chart, and
directions for making the power objects and
jewelry in the book. I've also included a list of
Bead Societies and a list of my favorite music to
bead by. Listen to the music and let yourself go
where the beads take you. Beads have the power to
open minds and heal hearts. What are we waiting
for? Let's bead together.

Part One:
THE MAGIC OF BEADS

"In our family we do beadwork to pay tribute to relatives who have passed on. Often I feel their presence when I sit down to bead. I can sense my mother, and sometimes I can hear her voice. She would hum or sing to give herself inspiration and go back into time; my grandmother was the very same way. So when I sit down for beadwork I do the same. I can hear them, and that gives me inspiration to do what I have to do."

—Drusilla Gould,

Native American bead artist

MY FIRST BEADS

This is a book about the power of beads.
Do you remember your first beads?

It's OK if you don't remember.
I'm going to share mine with you.

My grandmother gave me my first beads
when I was a small child.

They felt smooth and worn
from the touch of her fingers.

We took these beads everywhere with us ,
inside this little silk bag.

My grandmother kept her beads
in this bag, too.

My grandmother always dressed in black to
honor my grandfather, who lived in the spirit world.

One fall night while we were riding in the
back seat of my Uncle Jim's Chevrolet,
she taught me how to pray
with my beads.

The moon was fully round and yellow. It followed
our car like a big eye in the sky.

My grandmother told me the Art Father lived up there.
She said he was the father of all creation and she taught
me how to say his prayer while touching my beads.
"Art Father who art in heaven, hallowed bead thy name..."

Then there was the Hay Mary, Full of Grace.

My grandmother taught me to look for her in the woods,
under stones, and in the fields. We prayed
to Hay Mary with beads, too. Hay Mary
made plants and trees grow.

.

My grandmother and I spent a lot of time in the woods.
We picked mushrooms and wildflowers and we
carried them in a bundle in the fabric of her long skirt.

We took the beads into the woods with us.
We sat around a circle of stones and lit fires.
We took out our beads and we prayed.

One day, Hay Mary sat right down next to
us on a stone as we said our prayers.

My grandmother just looked at me
and smiled.

Every morning I stood on the bed and combed my
grandmother's long gray hair. It was soft and straight
like corn silk. It was the color of ashes from the fire.

I moved the comb slowly and gently and stopped when
I came to snarls. I watched her fingers move across
her beads and I felt safe inside.

When I was done, my grandmother put
her hair up in a bun.

I decorated it with tortoiseshell combs
from Italy. They were covered with white beads from
the sea. I thought these tiny white beads must be what
Art Father's moon looked like when he was a baby.

One day, the driveway was icy.

My grandmother fell down and broke her
hip. I wasn't sure what a hip was,
but she had to stay in bed
for a long time.

My grandmother showed me how to heal
her hip with beads.

We put our hands over the hurt
place and used the beads to call the Art Father
and the Hay Mary to this place in her body.
This made my grandmother feel
warm energy in her legs.

Then one day when I was only seven, everything changed.

My grandmother died during the night.
My mother said I wouldn't be going over to see
her anymore. I went to her house to get my beads,
but they were gone, too.

Every day I took a nap after lunch,
alone in my bedroom.

I didn't really sleep, but I liked having
quiet time alone, away from the adults. That was
when my grandmother started to visit me.

One day, I said: "I want my beads, Nonna."

She told me that my beads were gone.
"You have something far more precious than the beads.
You have the power of the beads inside of you and nobody
can take that away from you ever."

"I want you, Nonna."

"You have me inside of you, too, just like
the beads, I promise. Now listen to me and don't forget...
the magic is not in the beads alone, the magic
of the beads is in the Vision."

"Vision is knowing how to use the beads to see
with the eyes in your heart.

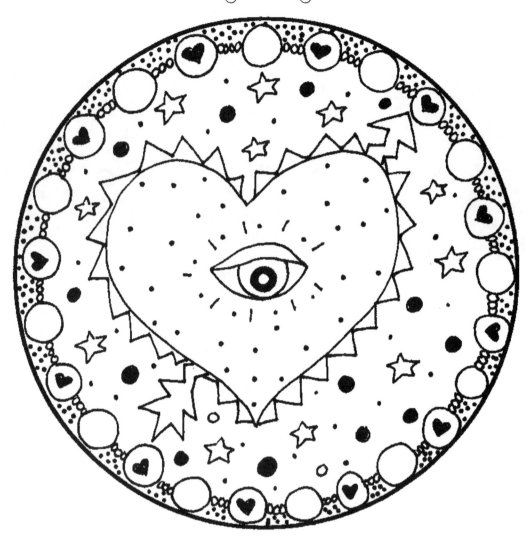

"These are God's favorite prayer beads.
Now go and share your beads with the world,
and know we are always connected."

The Universe
is Full of
magical things patiently
waiting
for our wits to grow
sharper.
- Eden
Phillips

THE BEAD CONNECTION

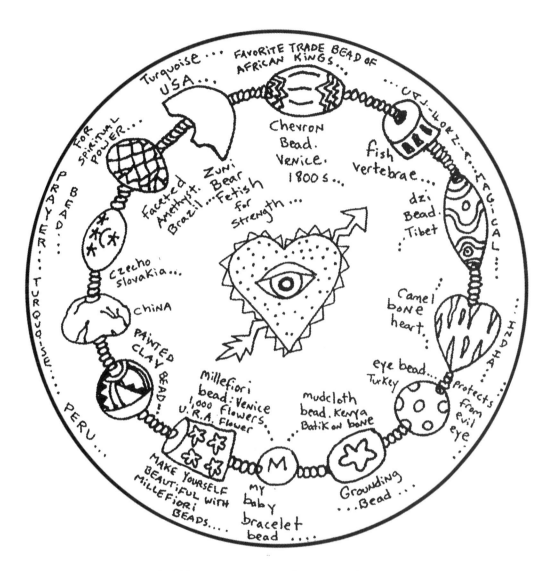

I'd like you to have these.
These are my beads.

Beads are everywhere you have ever been and
they are already waiting for you
at your next destination.

There is no getting away from beads,
so you might as well join them.

In the beginning, there was the Blessed Bead,
bearer of visions, colors, and charms.

You have known this bead before and you carry
the memory of its face deep inside of you.

Allow yourself to feel the attraction. You are not alone.

Human beings and beads have a long history together.
Physical contact arouses mystery and magnetism.
Priestesses wore beads. So did warriors, visionaries,
healers, and queens. Beads awaken archetypal
images within.

Beads embellish our collective memory.

Madonna wears beads. Cave women and cave men
wore beads. Jackie O. wore beads. So did
Pocahontas, Barbie, Jesus, and Cinderella.

I have powerful chemistry with beads. So do you.
It's no secret. You just might not know it yet.
There are many other people out there just like us.

One day, a bead just shows up. It happens
differently for each one of us. There is no rhyme or
reason to the beginning of this love affair.

Beads are the eyes of our soul looking back at us from the mirror. We cannot help but stare.

We are drawn in by color, shape, texture, eccentricity, and charm. We start daydreaming about beads. We start asking other people what they know about beads.
Next thing you know, we actually start pursuing beads on our own.

When a bead whispers your name, it is the sound of your soul calling collect. There is an urgency to make the connection.

The message is clear:
WE NEED TO BEAD TOGETHER.

At first, you will think you are
doing the choosing.

With time, you will come to understand
it is you who has been chosen.

Beads demand that you put all previous
plans aside and attend to the magic
of the moment. The present comes
in all colors, shapes, and sizes.

Let yourself go with the flow of primal attraction.
In the heat of the moment it's easy to lose our
heads. That's the whole idea.

It's a right brain seduction, this passion for beads.
Open your mind and have a multicullural,
many-faceted, homo-ancestral, intergalactic,
ethno-erotic, divinely inspired, lifelong
love affair with beads.

Beads are sensual creatures with questionable
backgrounds who oftentimes play hard to get. God
knows where these beads have been, or who
has been holding them before you.

A colorful history and a mysterious past
only make beads more desirable and
enhance their reputation.

Beads get shy around fast people who spend their lives chasing carrots.

This is why many people in our busy culture don't even know beads are alive.

Beads are gypsies: glittering, magical, and primitive hitchhikers. You slow down to take a look, and they attach themselves to your soul.

Make no mistake; you are the destination.

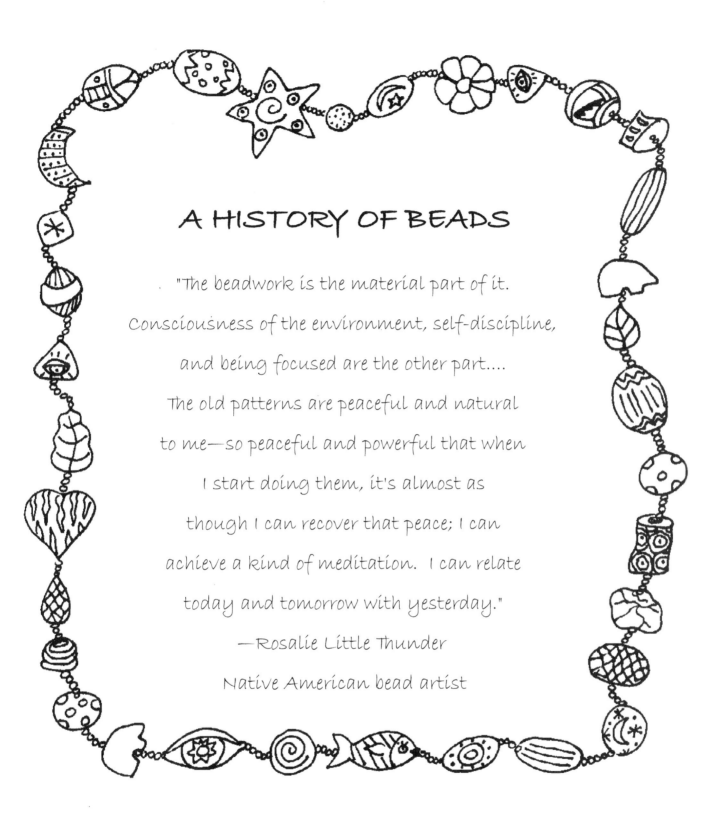

A HISTORY OF BEADS

"The beadwork is the material part of it.
Consciousness of the environment, self-discipline,
and being focused are the other part....
The old patterns are peaceful and natural
to me—so peaceful and powerful that when
I start doing them, it's almost as
though I can recover that peace; I can
achieve a kind of meditation. I can relate
today and tomorrow with yesterday."
—Rosalie Little Thunder
Native American bead artist

Begin to listen to the ancestral voices of beads.
They have a fascinating story to tell.

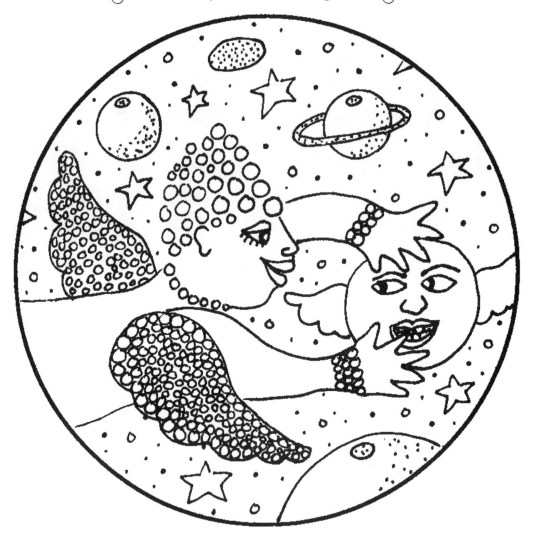

Allow a bead to anchor you in its history. It is your
history, too. Beads have the power to transport
us to other worlds if we are open to travel.

You know you're going back thousands of years when
you start to see beads made out of animal teeth,
bone, seeds, pebbles, and claws.

These beads belonged to our nomadic ancestors.

The ancients gave beads talismanic properties and used them in rituals to invoke divine protection, abundance, healing, and fertility.

Our ancestors believed that carving beads out of the bones, horns, and teeth of the animals they hunted gave them magical powers over the animals' souls.

Without supermarkets or insurance policies,
ancient people were faced with unique
survival challenges.

Primitive art was a voice that asked God for
protection and assistance. Beads were the words that
whispered in God's ears. Beads have always been a
direct connection between Mother Earth,
the spirit world, and humankind.

For thousands of years before patriarchal religions,
we worshiped a female deity in the form
of a great goddess.

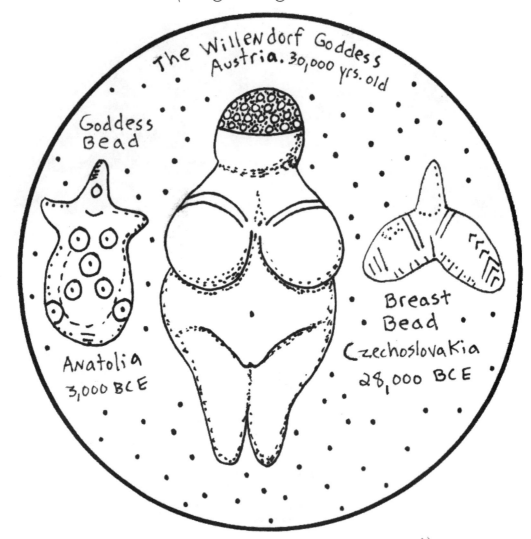

The Goddess was celebrated with beads.

In ancient Egypt, beads and amulets were used for protection and abundance. The Egyptians loved beads of gold, carnelian, lapis, and turquoise.

For them, colors had talismanic properties. Green symbolized the fertility of the earth. Carnelian awakened life energy. Lapis represented the sky and was referred to as the "heavenly stone."

The Egyptians used beads as a passport
to the afterworld.

They buried their dead with beads, covered their
mummies with beaded nets, and placed beads
under the eyelids of their deceased.

In Egypt, "sha" means luck, "sha sha" means bead.

It was thought that one's spirit would be welcomed
in the afterlife with open arms if it showed up
in beautiful beads.

Beads were also popular with Native Americans.
They used wampum beads (drilled quahog clam shells),
elk teeth, turquoise, and glass beads for money.

They used beaded images on clothing, cradle boards,
horses' tack, and ritual objects to express
social status and spiritual visions.

For their dead, Native Americans made spirit moccasins
with elaborately beaded soles.

The Tibetans embellished the soles of the shoes of their
dead with beautiful beads, too.
Perhaps the soul travels best dressed in beads.

Beads could walk before money could talk.
Long ago, explorers, merchants, and
adventurers never left home without their beads.

Venice, Italy, was the center of glass bead making
from 1200 to the 1800s. Telling the secrets of
the trade was a crime punishable by death.
Venetian beads were traded in places as far away
as North and South America, Asia, and Africa.

In North America, beads were traded for beaver pelts, land, and information crucial to the Europeans' survival in a new world.

In Asia, beads were traded for silks and spices.
In Africa, beads were traded for gold,
palm oil, and slaves.

In present-day Africa, beads are still used in healing, divination, and coming-of-age rituals.

Shamans wear ceremonial beaded necklaces and use beaded power objects. The Yoruba honor familial spirits with fantastic bead art. Zulu girls write beaded love letters to their suitors.

Beads have also been used for prayer throughout
the ages. Muslims, Buddhists, Catholics,
and Hindus all use prayer beads.

The root of the word "bead" actually means "prayer."
It is derived from the Anglo-Saxon "bidden"
(to pray), "bede" (prayer).

In Europe, rosaries were made of crushed rose petals.
Early Buddhist prayer beads were made from
the bones of enlightened monks.

Both roses and bones symbolize the transient
nature of this life.

In parts of Indonesia, beads are scattered around temples to invite divine blessings. Beads are sprinkled in rice fields to ensure abundant harvests.

As you can see, beads have a magical appeal that transcends time and culture.

The history of beads is as large as life itself.

Beads connect us to our ancestors. Beads give us
a sense of belonging in this world.

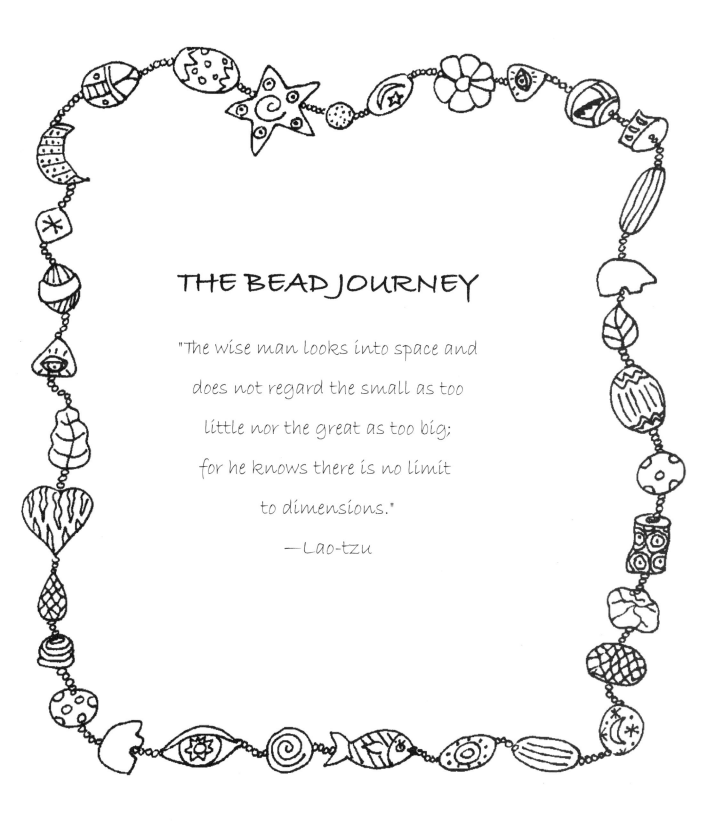

THE BEAD JOURNEY

"The wise man looks into space and
does not regard the small as too
little nor the great as too big;
for he knows there is no limit
to dimensions."

—Lao-tzu

Beads continue to inspire spirit
in modern times.

Present-day bead magic combines intention, faith,
and visualization into beautiful, wearable
prayers. We use beads to manifest miracles
and to make dreams come true.

I invite you to join me as we embark upon a
journey of intentional beading.

Come on, it's time to go to the Bead Room
and make your body a temple.

Sit down. Make yourself comfortable
and enjoy the view.

The circle is our sacred space. When we bead together, we
sit in a circle to connect our energy and to center
our power. Take a moment to quiet your mind.

Making jewelry is easy. We can all learn how.

Way before the word "artist" ever existed, people made their own jewelry. Deep inside of us, these ancient memories of creative connection still remain.

What makes a piece of jewelry magical
or sacred? You.

Close your eyes and state your intentions. Ask for
your vision and let the materials move you. Make
jewelry with soul. Breathe life into your art.

We have the power to transform our lives by beading
our intentions into sacred objects
and jewelry that we wear.

In turn, the bead, the charm, and the amulet have the power to awaken the energy of transformation within us.

Creating art with intention opens the door
to a world of DIVINE possibility, where all you
can imagine has already come true.

Beads take us on a journey spiraling from one world
into the next, leaving only the patterns of
our fingerprints behind.

The spiral is a vortex, a path, the very essence of our
creative DNA. We follow the thread of beads through
our fingers until we arrive at the place of inner vision.

When we vibrate with inner vision, ways of seeing
shift and the landscape of our being begins to change.

We arrive at an ancient fire surrounded by stones
and beads. This is the place our inner
artist calls home.

Remember, in ancient societies the artist was the healer,
the shaman, and the magician.

Give your inner artist permission to reach into
the earth and play with beads of fire.
Don't worry, you won't get burned.

The fire of imagination has its own story to tell.
Go ahead and open the book.

Bold
Elegant
Animated
Daring
Survivors

Beautiful
Empty
Awakened
Divine
Seeds

Because
Excavating
Awareness
Delivers
Serenity

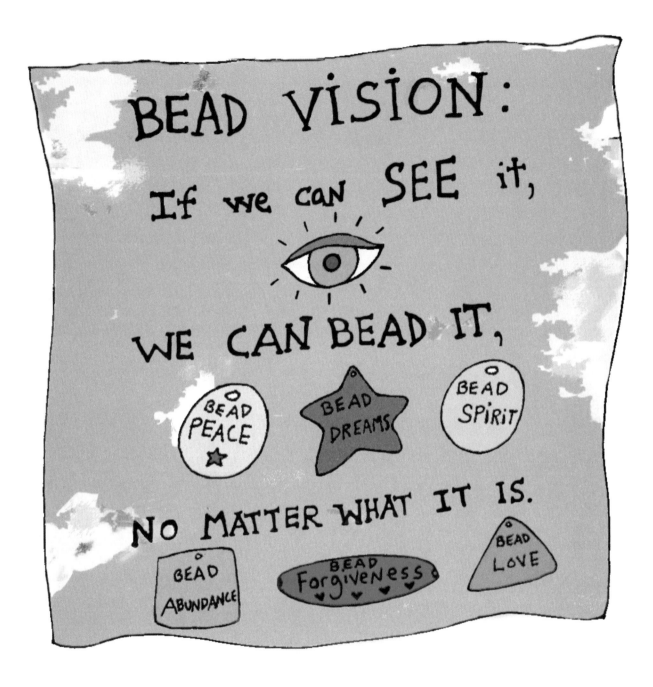

You are the Queen Bead!

What is it the Queen Desires?

Align Your Will with Divine Will and state your intentions here.

The World is Your Oyster
When You Bead With Treasures
From the Sea... ☆

°°° pearls are for faith & wisdom

shells are for protection, fertility,
& prosperity

Coral is for intuition &
creativity

For You

─ message in a bottle:

You Are the Treasure.

Materials are Miraculous!

-Bead on!

Glass

Glass is a liquid that becomes solid at room temperature. We heat it with fire. Glass goes with the flow, when things heat up and then it just chills. Transformation is the gift of glass. Glass reminds us of our fragility. Handle each. other with care.

Horn

Horn is for protection and manifestation. It is the physical body of the warrior energy within. Horn represents our visions taking form in this world. Use horn to focus your intentions and move ahead with clarity toward your goals & dreams.

Bone

Bone is a strong, porous substance that supports our bodies and protects our hearts, lungs, & brains. Bone symbolizes our connection to our ancestors. Bone represents the transient nature of life. Wear bone for connection to animal & ancestral power. When we live with reverence for our ancestors, our behavior honors both the Spirit World and the world we live in.

Clay

Clay is a gift from the earth. We come from the earth and to the earth, we shall return. Clay connects us to the energy of the Great Mother. Use clay to activate the Mother archetype within yourself. Move slowly through this busy world. Make time to rest, nurture, and rejuvenate yourself.

Shell

Shell is for protection, fertility, and abundance; all the things associated with a happy, stable home. Shell beads have been widely used for money in diverse cultures, all over the world. Use shell to manifest abundance, safety, and shelter for all beings. Then take the steps to make it happen.

Ostrich Egg Shell

Did you know there are beads made of ostrich egg shells? There are and i need their lesson every day. The egg symbolizes divine partnership, patience, and trust. Protect your dreams while they are growing and keep them to yourself. Egg shell keeps embryonic visions tightly sealed and protected from the outer environment. Trust that growth happens in the darkest of places.

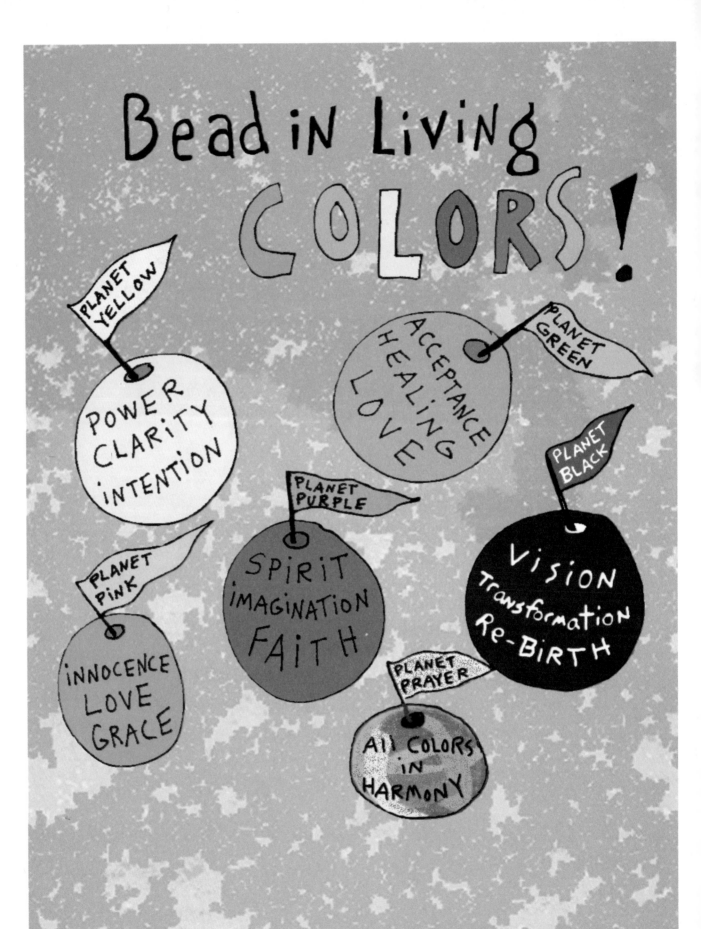

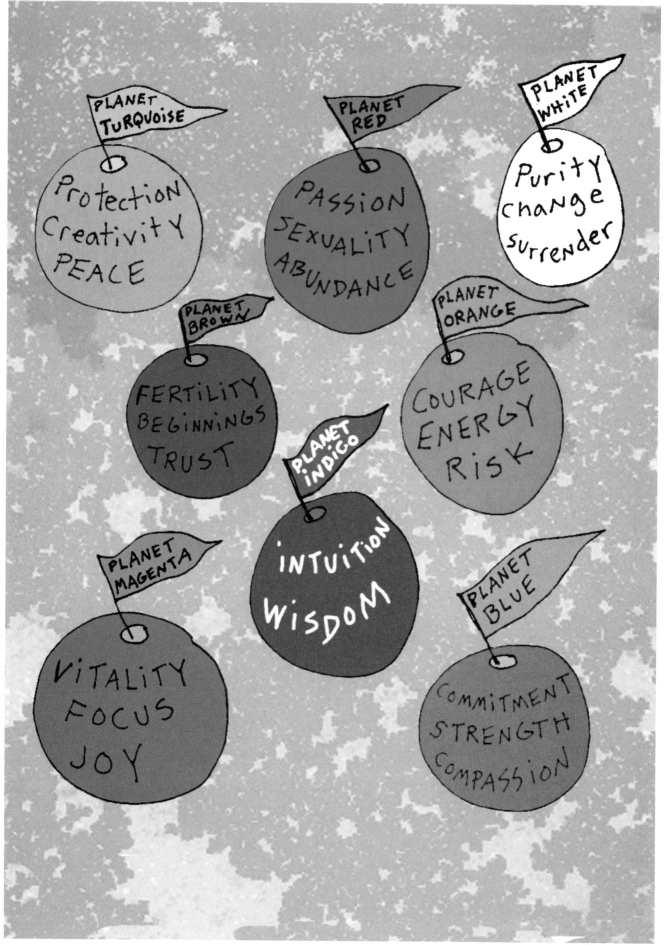

BEad
the change
You wish to see
in the world.

— Gandhi
(sort of)

In Native American tradition, Art is alive. Potters leave a crack in the pot, so that the "spirit" of the vessel may come and go. Weavers leave an oddly colored thread for the same purpose. When you make jewelry, you, too, can put a "spirit bead" in your design. This way, you can always keep an eye on your spirit.

Dzi Beads

Certain beads have magical reputations within their native cultures. Once their reputations get around, everyone wants them. Dzi beads are the sacred beads of Tibet. No one knows how old dzi beads really are, they simply refer to them as "ancient." Dzi beads are said to have fallen from the heavens...

It's raining BEADS!

In Tibet...
...Turquoise is sacred...
...Coral is sacred....
...Life is sacred...
Free Tibet.....
Amber is sacred...
Jewelry is sacred...

Bodom Beads

Bodom beads are the sacred powder glass beads of Ghana. They are mostly yellow beads with swirls, dots, and flowing designs. The more worn and chipped they are, the more valuable. Popular legend says bodom beads originated by springing forth from the Earth.

GARDEN OF
BEADEN
PICK YOUR OWN
BODOM BEADS

imagination is the real trip.
The Earth is Alive.
Close Your eyes and go inside.
Your Mother's beads will heal You.

(T)(H)(A)(N)(K)(S)(M)(O)(M)

Amber O - for healing
Amethyst O - for spirit
Bloodstone O - for courage
Carnelian O - for inspiration
Chrysoprase O - for acceptance
Citrine O - for Abundance
Garnet O - for Health
Hematite O - for Grounding
Jade O - for dreams
Jasper O - for Joy
Labradorite O - for strength

Lapis Lazuli O - for wisdom
Malachite O - for change
Moonstone O - for New beginnings
Peridot O - for friendship
Quartz O - for Power
Rose Quartz O - for Love
Tiger Eye O - for clarity
Turquoise O - for Peace, Protection, & Creativity
silver O - for balance
Copper O - for harmony
gold O - for purity

The Shapes of Beads Carry Hidden Meanings

○ The circle represents wholeness, unity, movement, and divine protection. It symbolizes the journey of becoming one's authentic self in the world. Choose round beads with intentions of healing and fulfilling your life's purpose. We come "full circle" when we are able to give back to others and be of service to the world.

☐ The square represents grounding and stability. It embodies the strength to make your plan and the will to follow it through. Choose square beads to invoke the power of manifestation on the physical plane. You are ready to build your dreams on solid ground.

△ The triangle contains your dreams and visions. The downward pointing triangle symbolizes female intuition, fertility, and earth based spirituality. The upward pointing triangle represents focused energy and creativity. The three sides of the triangle represent your dream, your actions toward making it real, and the Divine guidance that supports you in every step of your process.

◎ The spiral represents growth, change, and the Natural energy of the universe moving from one state into another. Choose spiral shaped beads or beads with a spiral motif to make the process of growth & transformation a conscious journey. Ask yourself where it is you see yourself going and what it is you are being asked to leave behind.

Eye Beads

Eye beads are magical beads found in many cultures. They are especially popular in the Middle East. They consist of a dot or a dot in a circle motif, representative of an eye. They are used to protect the wearer from the unwanted influences of the "evil eye." I have seen eye beads on beautiful women in Italy, on donkeys in Turkey, on boats in Portugal, on buses in Mexico, and pinned to Cape Verdean babies' t-shirts on Cape Cod. Keep your eyes open. Eye beads are everywhere!

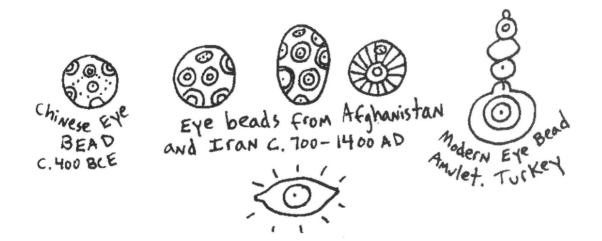

Chinese Eye Bead C. 400 BCE

Eye beads from Afghanistan and Iran C. 700-1400 AD

Modern Eye Bead Amulet, Turkey

"What is the 'Evil Eye,' anyway?"

Before the concept of the "evil eye" ever existed, there were the "eyes of the Goddess." The eyes of the Goddess sprang from the art of prehistoric Goddess worship and Earth based spirituality. The eyes of the Goddess invoked the interconnectedness of all life, female power, healing, and community. These are the eyes of the Goddess:

Eyes of the Goddess (Spain, 3,000 BCE)

Eye Goddess (Syria 3,000 BCE)

When patriarchal religions became the rage, the eyes of the Goddess were absorbed into the symbolism of the evil eye. I'm still not exactly sure how to describe an evil eye. i think it's an eye that could belong to any one of us, male or female. Evil eyes show up in all kinds of bodies with eyes wide open and hearts tightly closed. Things like pollution, racism, and greed are real life visions of the evil eye. We wear eye beads to remind ourselves to open our hearts each morning as soon as we open our eyes. When we all do this every day, we won't need to worry about evil eyes anymore. 👁

Don't be Afraid to Use Your Charms

HAND:
healing...
creativity...
divine protection

Butterfly:
Soul...
Re-birth...

Arrowhead:
Focus...
PERSEVERANCE

SCARAB:
Re-birth...
(Egyptian)

FEATHER:
Grace...
NON-attachment
Serenity

FISH:
Faith...
Fertility

Pi Disk:
Heaven...
Transcendence...
Surrender...

Goddess:
POWER...
CHANGE...
Vision...

Eye of Horus:
HEALTH...
PROSPERITY...
(EGYPTIAN)

To Get What You Want in this World...

BUDDHA: peace... Compassion...

KOKOPELLI: Fertility...

ZUNI BEAR: strength...

EYES of the Goddess: MANIFESTATION, RELATIONSHIP, VISION

DOLPHIN: JOY... PLAY... MAGIC...

FROG: Fertility... speaking out...

BEE: Goddess Power... Creative Community...

Crescent Moon: CHANGE...

SPIDER: creativity...

Angel: Divine Protection...

SHELL: sexuality

OWL: wisdom...

WISHBONE: DREAMS...

ANKH: Life Power... ABUNDANCE... (Egypt)

TURTLE: MOTHER EARTH (NATIVE AMERICAN)... PATIENCE...

YIN YANG: BALANCE...

BUFFALO: Abundance... (Native American)

SNAKE: LIFE FORCE... transformation...

LADY BUG: SUCCESS... LUCK...

HEART: Love...

STAR: Dreams... Divine Grace...

CROSS: Pre-christian: FERTILITY... christian: PROTECTION

Tibetan Prayer Box: DIVINE GUIDANCE...

IN Japan, people sometimes ask the question: "What is your charm point?" A charm point is the thing unique to you that attracts others.... What is yours?

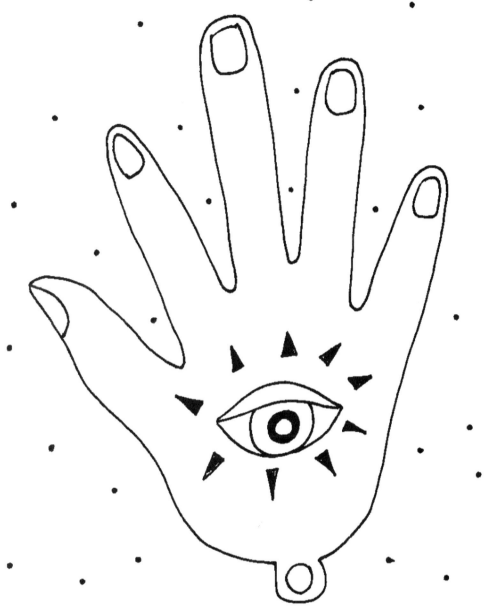

What is it you wish to create?
Envision it in Your Mind's eye.
The magic is in Your hands.

LAW #1 of BEAD MANIFESTATION:

POWER

The POWER is WITHIN You!

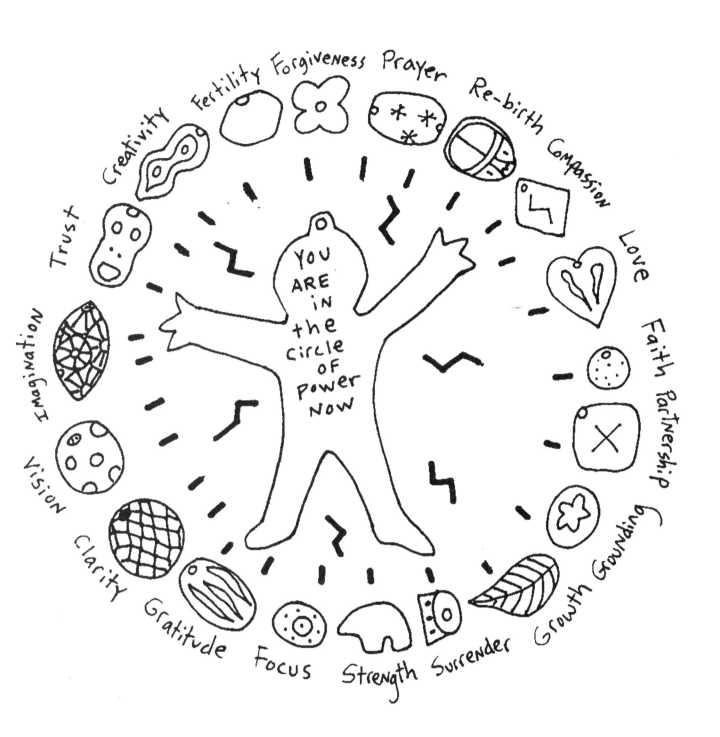

Creativity Fertility Forgiveness Prayer Re-birth Compassion Love Faith Partnership Grounding Growth Surrender Strength Focus Gratitude Clarity Vision Imagination Trust

YOU ARE iN the circle OF POWER NOW

LAW # 2 of BEAD MANIFESTATION:

ENERGY FOLLOWS THOUGHT

FOCUS YOUR ENERGY AND WATCH IT GROW!

-Powerful Thought- :Electric Energy-

Strength   Love   Dreams   Vision

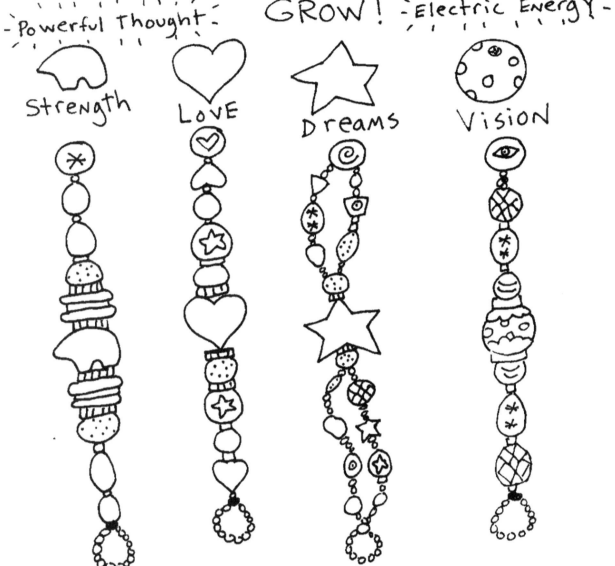

Your Manifestation Bracelet is
making miracles happen! So Are You!
keep Your Eye on the
BEAD!

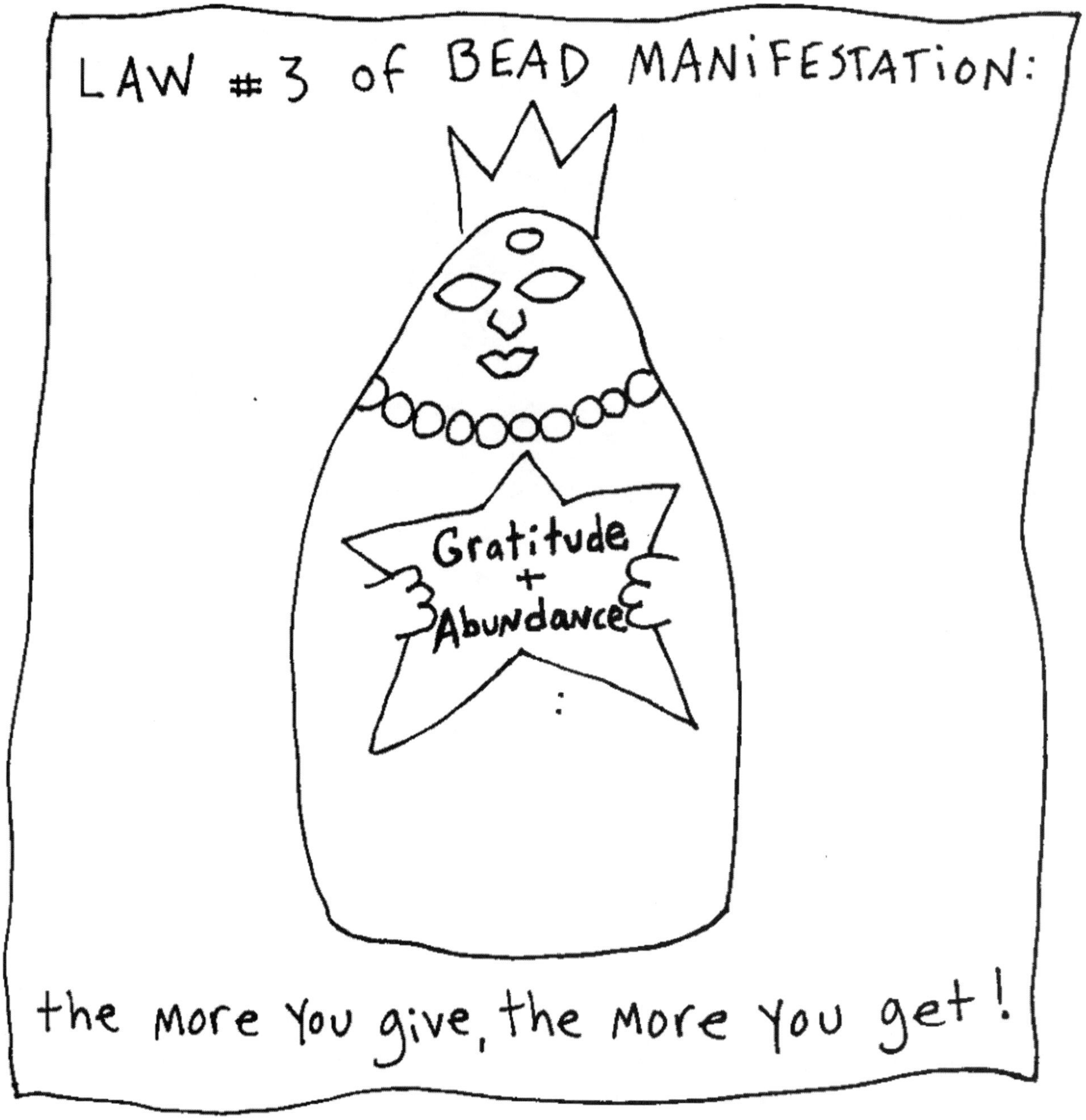

LAW #3 of BEAD MANIFESTATION:

Gratitude
+
Abundance

the more you give, the more you get!

SAY THANK YOU IN ADVANCE ♥

YOUR
ABUNDANCE
NECKLACE
is
HERE

OPEN UP YOUR ARMS TO RECEIVE.
THE UNIVERSE IS A GENEROUS PLACE.
GRACIAS · MERCI · DOMO ARIGATO · GRAZIE
DE NADA · DE RIEN · DŌ ITASHIMASHITE · PREGO
THANK YOU ♥ YOU'RE WELCOME ♥ THANK YOU

LAW # 4 of BEAD MANIFESTATION:

DREAM

If you can see it, you can BEad it.

You Are the Weaver of Your Own Destiny

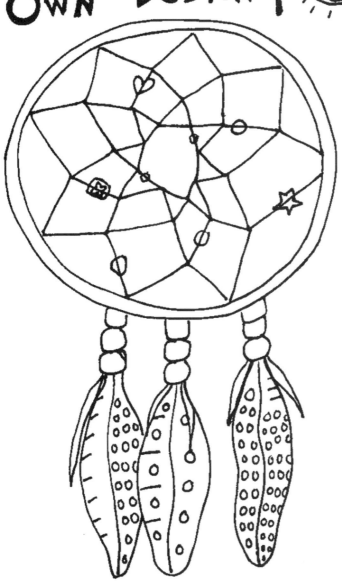

Use your Dream Catcher to Make Dreams Reality

LAW # 5 of BEAD MANIFESTATION:

TRUST
CHANGE

TRUST THE INVISIBLE ENERGY THAT BRINGS CHANGE.

CHANGE is iN THE AiR. BREATHE DEEPLY.
MAKE A BEAD RATTLE TO FiND YOUR
NEW RHYTHM.

TRUST A FRiEND.
THERE iS A WHOLE UNiVERSE OUT THERE
WAiTiNG FOR YOU TO PLAY.

LAW # 6 of BEAD MANIFESTATION:

GRACE

You Are Full of GRACE.

THIS IS A SPIRIT DOLL. HER NAME IS GRACE

GRACE IS A GIFT OF DIVINE LOVE. SHE SHOWS UP WHEN WE LEAST EXPECT HER AND SHE FILLS OUR EMPTY SPACES. GRACE IS MADE OF BEADS. ART IS AN ACT OF GRACE.

LAW # 7 of BEAD MANIFESTATION:

HEALING

You Are A Channel For Healing Energy

TUNE into THE PULSE OF THE PLANET.
BEad a force of LOVE and HEALING...

Prayer Flags send powerful prayers out into
the world. One image can open a heart.
One word can change a mind. One bead
can heal a Spirit. Never underestimate
the POWER of Art.

LAW # 8 of BEAD MANIFESTATION:

LOVE

If it's not Love, throw it away....

BEad LOVE.

After all, what else is there to bead?
If it's not love, put it in Your "God Gourd"
and wait for a Miracle.

Beaded God Gourd:
Put Your Fears in Now

Beaded God Gourd
Full of Grace

The God Gourd is a sacred vessel that
takes all our fears and turns them
into LOVE. when the love is ready, take
it out and spread it around. Then when
Your vessel is empty, fill it with Grace.
She's always looking for a place to stay.

Teach Children to Love all Colors & Cultures of Beads

BEADS CELEBRATE OUR DELICIOUS DIVERSITY!

LATINO is Luscious

Female is Fabulous

BALINESE is BEAUTIFUL

Children are Cherished

American is Amazing

Italian is Intriguing

Gay is Good

African is Awesome

MALE is Miraculous

Elderly is Elegant

BEAD LOVE IN THE WORLD

All colors Are cool

Beads Have Holes.
So do we.

The hole is the place where Spirit enters and exits the bead. Sometimes our wounds are the holes through which Spirit enters & exits us. Things like betrayal, hatred, and greed can make big holes... i don't know why exactly but maybe it's because forgiveness is so HUGE.... Hopefully, one day we will remember to stay OPEN to SPIRIT all the time, and we won't need our wounds anymore to remind us.

Keep your Spirit Hole open!

We Are All Human Beads...
vertebrae strung together on sacred spinal cords

spinal cord

hole

— your vertebrae are beads

"Excuse me, Are you a human bead or a prayer in disguise?"

Um... i was wondering... if the word "bead" means "prayer" and we are all beads, does that make us all prayers in disguise? And if so, do we bring prayer into the public schools just by showing up each morning? i hope so. (and i hope no one gets arrested.)

Human Beads Are The Most Magical
Beads of all...Human Beads have
imagination. Human beads can BEad
anything at all... Sometimes it's
just a matter of knowing what it is
you want to BEad... ☆ and
then believing in your power.

You Can
Trust
the
QUEEN

"The POWER is in the VISION."
When we Know what we want

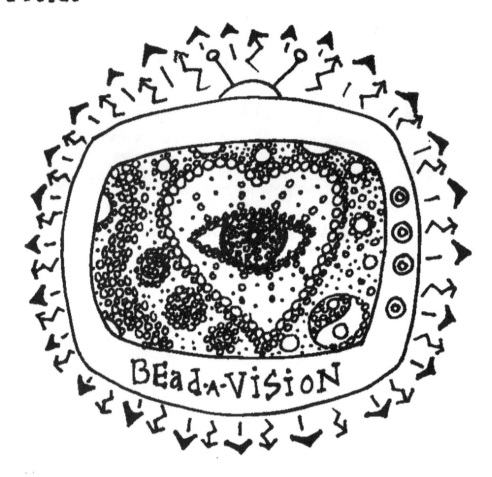

BEad-A-VISION

to BEad, we focus our vision
and send powerful energy
waves out to the Universe.
Let the Divine Dialogue begin!

The Universe supports Bead Vision with generous gifts.

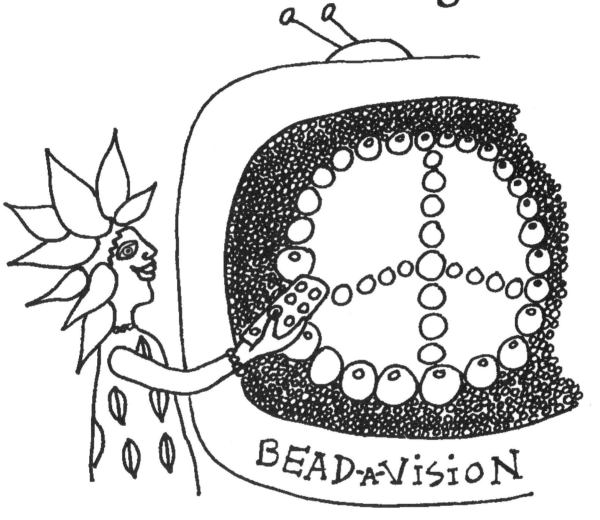

BEAD-A-VISION

Go ahead and show SPIRIT what's on your mind...

Once you start broadcasting your vision

in the world, all kinds of help will appear to support your show. You are now practicing Bead Magic in your own home, where blessings wear beads and **miracles happen.**

WHeN we change

our thoughts, the world follows.

IN Chinese, the character for "bead"
and "pupil of the eye" are one and
the same.

We use our eyes to see the world
as it is...

We use our beads to see with
the mind's eye and to manifest
change with our vision.

When You're ready,
go ahead and change...

The Secret
INNeR
Language
of
BEADS

Bead-A-VisioN

the channel. We're going
to close this book now and go
meet some bead friends.

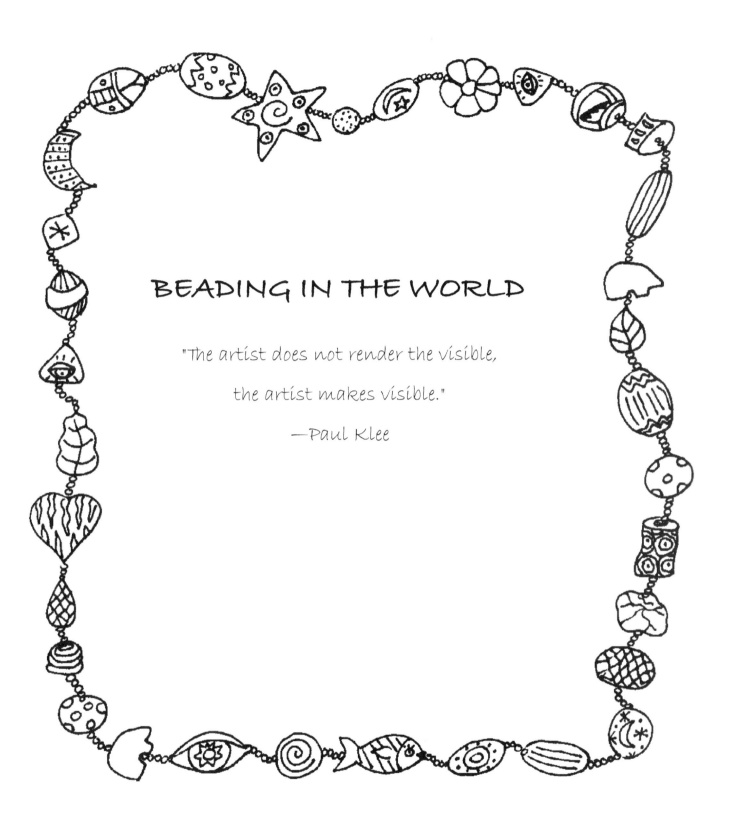

BEADING IN THE WORLD

"The artist does not render the visible,

the artist makes visible."

—Paul Klee

This is my friend Susan. Susan is a true
bead lover. She is my bead mentor.

Susan travels across country in a truck full of beads,
amulets, charms, and stones. She builds fabulous
altars in hotel rooms and sells them at bead
shows. I suggest you find a bead mentor
like Susan and go along for the ride.

Susan introduced me to Ava. Ava's grandmother
introduced her to beads, too. Ava created her own
traveling bead show, called the Whole Bead Show.

The Whole Bead Show is a fabulous place to learn
about beads, meet bead makers and bead collectors,
and become a bead lover yourself.

Kathy "Eagle Mother" taught me how to make dream catchers and rattles. Kathy's bead studio is in the New England woods, surrounded by birds, chipmunks, and the long silences of nature.

Kathy makes her own glass beads. She also makes sacred ceremonial and healing objects with bones, beads, hide, wood, shells, and feathers.

These are the teachers from the Heritage School in Charlton, Massachusetts. They love beads so much, they may be borderline beadaholics.

When my niece, Emily, was in third grade, they invited me to come to school and bring my beads. Beads make school an adventure!

Gabrielle is another amazing bead lover. Gabrielle received a millefiori bead in the mail one day and fell head over heels in love. Gabrielle's bead collection grew to such a size that she opened her own bead museum!

The Bead Museum is in Glendale, Arizona. When I visited, they were putting on a fashion show, featuring the beads, clothing, and cultural traditions of 52 different countries!

Cheryl is the director of the Bead Museum. Cheryl was working at a hospital in South Africa, when a patient gave her a beautiful strand of beads, and she caught the bead fever herself.

Cheryl's friend Judy is an artist and social activist who uses beads to create community projects and healing rituals. Judy's bead work brings awareness to our connection to the Earth, native cultures, our ancestors, and one another.

Betty is a 74-year-old jewelry designer, great-grandmother, and potter who lives in the desert. Betty's eyes are full of sparkle and charm. So is her bead work.

Betty uses Mojave symbols in her beaded necklaces and capes. The turtle, the frog, and the snake appear as sacred messengers from the Spirit world. In 1995, Betty was named a Living Treasure by the state of Arizona for her inspirational art.

Meet Karen and David. Karen and David run
Beads on Wheels, a traveling glass bead making
studio that brings beads to teenagers at risk all
across the United States. Karen and David dream
of creating an art camp for families at risk.

We are all at risk in a world where Art is not
a priority.

Art heals.

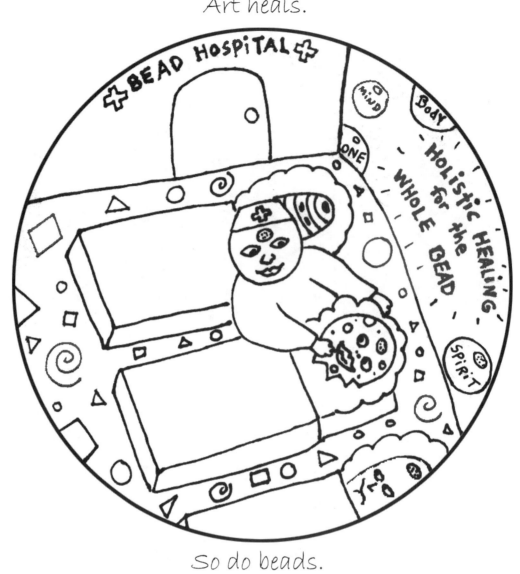

So do beads.

When we bead, our brain chemistry actually changes.
We enter a peaceful, relaxed state that rejuvenates
body, mind, and spirit.

Healing is a creative act.
Get in bed and let yourself BEad.

Invite a friend over to bead in bed, or bring
a bouquet of beads to a loved one.

Bedside beading at home and in the hospital
is both creative and curative.
Beads are good medicine.

Beads give us a three-dimensional voice to explore
our lows and vibrant colors to celebrate our highs.

Beads have holes for when we're in the middle.
Beads remind us that each season has its own color
and purpose.

Sometimes we mistake depression for hunger.

What good is a full belly if your spirit is starving?
Beads are soul food. They look so good,
we can eat them with our eyes.

It is only through setting our beads free that we learn to speak their language.

Begin each day with a bowl of beads.

Bring beads with you to bless new beginnings,
give thanks, make magic, and reclaim
rites of passage.

Go out into the world and commit spontaneous acts of public embellishment.

Bead grey statues, goddess gardens, and glittering worlds of possibility.

When you bead in public places, people will gather like bees and begin to buzz around.

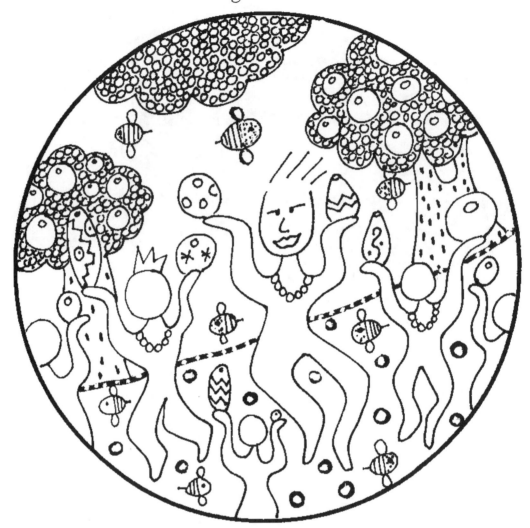

Go ahead and invite them to bead.

Bead high schools, sand castles, snowmen,
and saints.

Bead beautiful bridges between Believing
and Becoming. Then cross over into Being together.

Bead seeds of color, culture, creativity,
and community,

and plant them in growing minds.

Bead a nonconformist.

Bead magical suitcases and plan bead trips.
Let your imagination be your guide.

Bead wanderlust, wardrobes, and wheelchairs.

Bead canes, Christmas trees, cakes, and crutches.
Bead Buddhas in blue on the beach.

Bead to raise awareness, raise spirits, and raise money.

Bead museums, art camps, and bead dreams
are not built in a day.

Bead seeds of hope in dark pockets.

In time, your beads will sprout wings.

Bead cradles of compassion in unquiet corners.

Bead still and listen until the heartbeat of the
earth becomes one with your own.
Then bead this inner rhythm.

Don't bead attached to people and events that are beyond your control.

Bead what you came here to bead: YOURSELF.

Bead as if today were your last day on earth.

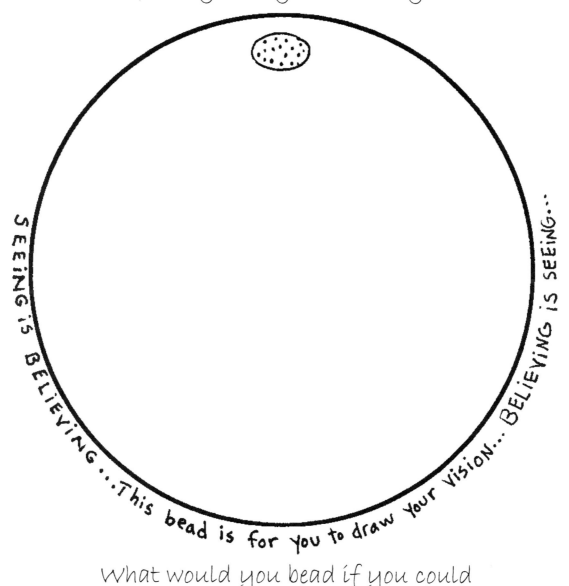

SEEING is BELIEVING...This bead is for you to draw your vision... BELIEVING is SEEING...

What would you bead if you could
bead anything at all?

Bead until your heart opens so wide that it becomes
a window through which everything comes alive.

Take care of each other. That is why we are here.
Beads celebrate the connection.

It is my hope this book has changed the way
you look at beads.

Maybe if we can look at beads in a new way, we
can see ourselves in a new light and this
will change the way we look at others.

Maybe we can bead a whole new world.

The End

Part Two:

BEAD HERE NOW

"The craft of questions, the craft of stories,
the craft of hands—
all these are the making of something and
that something is the soul."
—Clarissa Pinkola Estes

MY FAVORITE BEADS

Powder glass beads....
(Ghana)

Chevrons...
(older-Venice,
newer-Czechoslovakia,
India)

Eye beads....
(Venice, China,
Turkey, & India)

Ostrich egg shell beads...
...and cowrie shell beads...
(Kenya)

African trade beads...

Crystal and glass rondelles....
(Czechoslovakia)

Seed beads...
(Czechoslovakia)

Turquoise bears, scarabs, and stars...
(China, American Southwest, Africa)

. . . .

Peruvian beads....

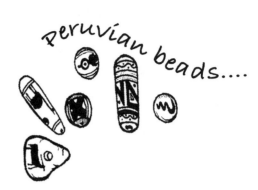

czech glass beads...

Spacer beads...
(Silver-Bali,
metal rings-Africa)

Horn beads....
(Philippines)

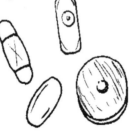

Venetian millefiori beads....

Bone beads...
(India, Kenya,
& Philippines)

Faceted stone beads.....
(amethyst, peridot,
citrine)

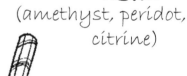

cornaline d'Alleppo....
(White hearts)

Silver and metal beads....
(India, Nepal, Thailand, & Bali)

Bodom beads...

Coconut husk beads...
(Africa)

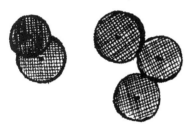

Metal Hieshi spacers

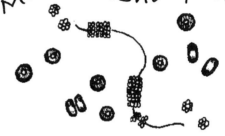

Swarovski Austrian crystal beads....

Crow beads...

TOOLS AND SUPPLIES

Tools you will need for projects in this book

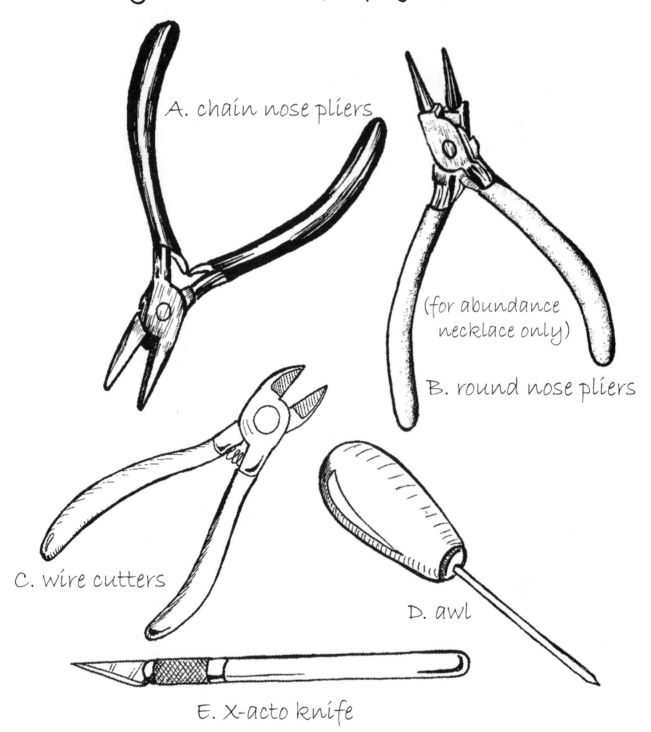

A. chain nose pliers

(for abundance necklace only)

B. round nose pliers

C. wire cutters

D. awl

E. X-acto knife

Supplies you will need

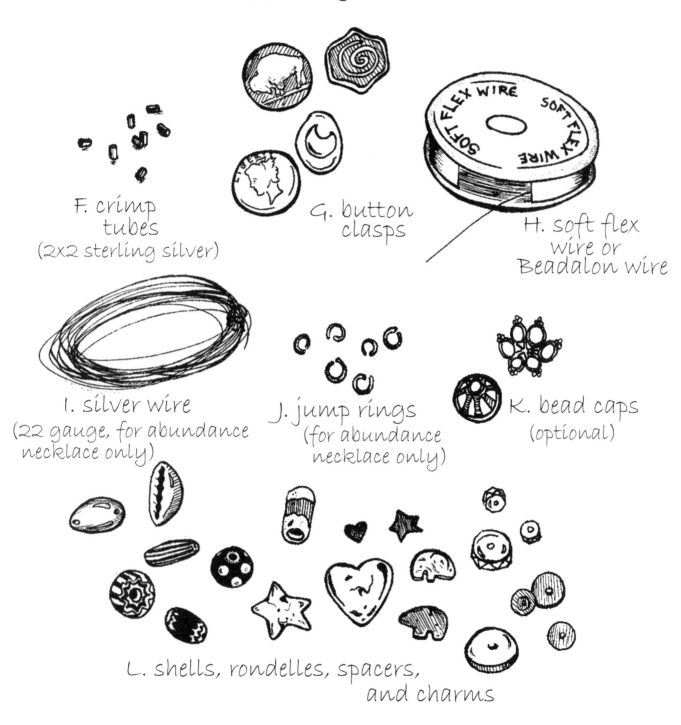

F. crimp tubes
(2x2 sterling silver)

G. button clasps

H. soft flex wire or Beadalon wire

I. silver wire
(22 gauge, for abundance necklace only)

J. jump rings
(for abundance necklace only)

K. bead caps
(optional)

L. shells, rondelles, spacers, and charms

My Favorite Music To Bead By

This is a list of some of my favorite music to bead by. It is a page of gratitude for the journeys of imagination each artist has inspired in me. The artists and their sounds are as diverse as the beads themselves. When we bead to music, we open ourselves up to the rhythms and flow of the invisible world, and we lose ourselves in the pure vibration of the creative experience. This is the place of healing where creative visions flow from our inner world. It is my hope that you take many bead trips to this sweet place and begin to make it your home. Add your own music to this list and begin to bead your own story.

Joan Armatrading—Greatist Hits
Shawn Colvin—Steady On,
     A Few Small Repairs
Sheila Chandra—Quiet
Miles Davis—Kind of Blue
Jimmy Cliff—Special
Manu Dibango—Wakafrica
Mickey Hart- Planet Drum
Angelique Kidjo—Logozo
Youssou N'Dour, Joko—From Village
     To Town
Joni Mitchell—Hejira

Paula Cole—This Fire
Boat People—Jackalope
One World—Putumayo Presents
Les Nubians—Princesses Nubians
Samite—Stars to Share
Carlos Santana—Supernatural
Raphael—Music to Disappear In
Virginia Rodriguez—Nos
The Story—Angel in the House
Neil Young—Comes A Time
Emmylou Harris—Wrecking Ball

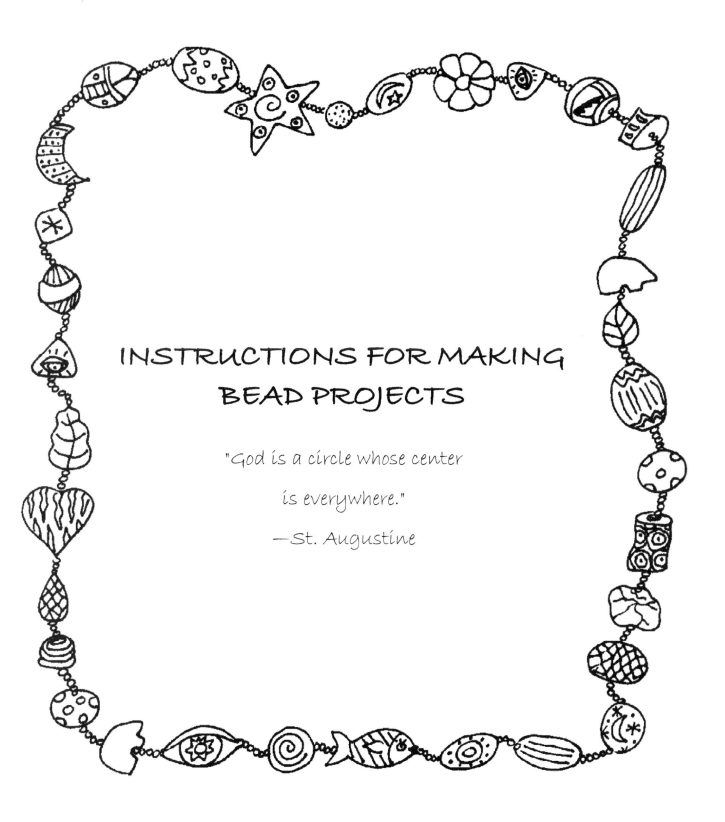

INSTRUCTIONS FOR MAKING BEAD PROJECTS

"God is a circle whose center

is everywhere."

—St. Augustine

The Power Circle and Ritual

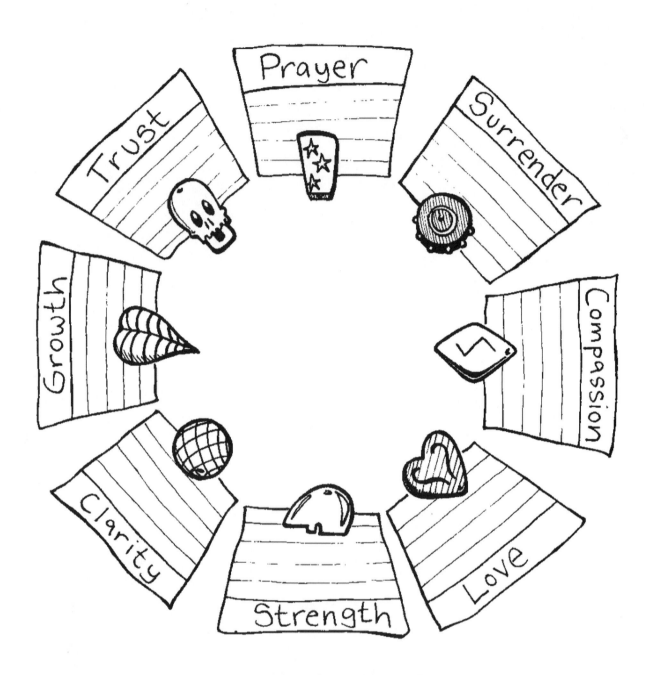

Law #1 of Bead Manifestation:
The Power Is Within You!
Key word: POWER
Bead project #1: The Power Circle
Supplies: beads, index cards, paper, paints, water, and brushes or markers

The circle is sacred space. It represents a timeless reality with no beginning and no end. The timeless realm is our place of creation where we receive and plant the seeds of our dreams. The circle is a place of wholeness and inner vision. Ancient stone circles in England remind us of the power of this form. In Native American culture, medicine wheels are circular; so are kivas and teepees. In Tibetan tradition, mandalas are circular, and so is the wheel of life. In both Christian and Eastern traditions, halos and rosaries are circular forms. Renaissance cathedral domes and round stained-glass windows create a feeling of sanctuary. In nature, the earth itself is perhaps the universal template for our cross-cultural devotion to the sacred circle.

We visit the circle for meditation, divine inspiration, and guidance. Create your own power circle with beads. It may be large enough to include a group of people or small enough to fit on top of your altar. It may be outside in your garden or inside your house. Write power words on paper cards or stones and place each word underneath a bead in your circle.

Power Bead Ritual: I like to keep my power circle full of paper, markers, crayons, paint, and art supplies. If I am meditating with a group, I put paper, water, and brushes in front of each participant before we begin our meditation. At this point the power words are lying facedown under beads in the circle. I ask each participant to choose a word and a bead. After reading the word, I ask them to put the card facedown and hold the bead in their hands.

I explain that we will be meditating for 20 minutes, focusing on our breath and our power word. Whenever we get lost in thought or stray from our meditation, we are to return to our word, our bead, and our breath. I then explain that when 20 minutes are up, I will sound a bell at which time we will begin to draw freely any images that came up for us during or after the meditation. If you have no images, this is OK. Just begin to draw or paint and trust the process as it unfolds.

We begin the meditation by saying "We now invite the Spirit of Art and Healing into our circle. We surrender all plans, all judgments, agendas, and worries in order to be present to the power of this moment. Our intention is to begin in this moment to listen to the voice of Spirit within ourselves and have faith in her divine presence. Spirit knows exactly what it is we need to begin living our life's purpose and fulfilling our healing journey. We now open our hearts to listen to her voice."

When we are finished drawing, I explain that we are now going to share our drawings and if anyone does not wish to participate, this is fine. I give the participants blank cards to write on. We walk around in silence, looking at each other's drawings. This is not a critique, rather it is a power walk. We ask ourselves what powers we observe in another's drawing and silently write one-word observations on our cards, and leave them next to the drawings.

When we are done, we return to the group and discuss our experience of the meditation and our images. We share our original power word and the power words seen by the observers. The purpose of the observers' power words is to make us aware of powers that others perceive in us that we may not be aware of in ourselves. Again, participation is voluntary. Then each participant chooses one of the power words to be her/his new name for the duration of the group. If you like, this whole exercise can also be done alone.

The Manifestation Bracelet and Ritual

Law #2 of Bead Manifestation:
Energy Follows Thought
Key word: FOCUS
Bead project #2: The Manifestation Bracelet

The manifestation bracelet represents your power to focus your mind to manifest miracles. It acts as a conduit between your thoughts, the divine, and manifestation in the physical realm. If you listen to the wisdom of the second law, "energy follows thought," then you understand that right now your energy is causing the object of your attention to grow to fruition in your life. Therefore, it is of utmost importance to focus your thoughts on the most positive and detailed life vision you wish to manifest.

Manifestation Bead Ritual: Draw a picture in detail of what it is you wish to create in your life. Then choose beads to represent each detail. Bead each element into your manifestation bracelet. FOCUS. If you are in a group, choose a partner and tell her about each detail in your life/bracelet as if it were a reality right now in the present moment. Have your partner introduce you to the larger group, by showing your bracelet and speaking of your life, as you see it.

Then participate in a "blessing of the bracelets" ritual. In this ritual we put the bracelets on our altar and shower them with water for life, flower petals for faith, and corn for fertility. Send your words out to the universe and make room to harvest your dreams!

Making Your Manifestation Bracelet

Tools: chain nose pliers, awl, scissors

Supplies: Softflex or Beadlon wire, beads, button style clasp, (1) 2x2 crimp tube, Bali style spacers or African metal ring bead caps (optional), crystal or glass rondelles (optional)

Steps

A. Choose a "power word" for your bracelet that you wish to embody.

B. Cut the wire 2x the length of your wrist plus 3 inches for finishing.

C. String enough seed beads onto the wire to make a loop that will fit snugly around your button clasp. String a bead through both ends of the wire and slip it down the wires until it secures the loop. This will create a double-strand bracelet form with a loop at the end. (fig. 1)

D. Check to see that your button clasp fits snugly through this loop before you continue further. This is to ensure that your bracelet will not fall off when you are wearing it. (fig. 2)

E. Decide if you want to string one solid strand of beads as in the Strength, Love, and Vision bracelets (p. 111), or if you want two separate strands that join in the center as in the Dreams bracelet (p. 111).

F. Begin to string your beads. Determine the center of your bracelet by forming the wire around your wrist and matching the center bead with the center of your wrist. (fig. 3)

G. When you have beaded equal distances on either side of the center, your bracelet should be the correct length. Fold the bracelet around your wrist to try it on as in figure 3. If the size is correct, you are ready to finish it.

H. Slip both ends of the wires through the crimp tube and slip the crimp tube onto the wire. (fig. 4)

I. Then slip the wires through the wire loop on the back of your button clasp. (fig. 5)

J. Now loop the wires back around through the crimp tube in the opposite direction. (fig. 6)

K. Insert the awl into the center of the wire loop and clamp the chain nose pliers onto the ends of the protruding wires. (fig. 7) Hold the awl firmly in one hand and pull the wires with the pliers in the other hand, creating tension. This will shorten the space around the button and tightly fasten it to the wire. (fig. 8)

L. When the button is tightly fastened, remove the awl and clamp the crimp tube tightly with the chain nose pliers. (fig. 9)

M. Cut off the excess wire with fingernail clippers. Your bracelet is finished.

1.

2.

3.

4.

5.

6.

7.

8.

9.

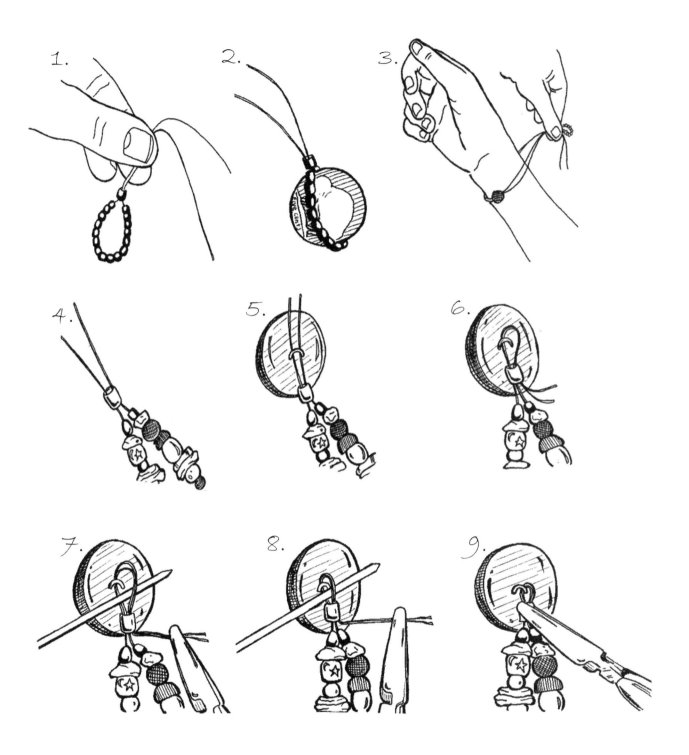

The Abundance Necklace and Ritual

Law #3 of Bead Manifestation:
The More You Give, the More You Get
Key words: GRATITUDE, ABUNDANCE
Bead project #3: The Abundance Necklace

The more grateful we are for all of our blessings, the more room we make for additional blessings in our lives. The abundance necklace is a physical representation of all we are thankful for. It may be made with just beads or with beads and charms. In either case, you choose charms or beads to represent your blessings. Make sure to thank the universe in advance for all the details that haven't yet appeared on the physical plane. This will speed up their arrival.

Abundance Bead Ritual: Keep a bowl of beads on your kitchen table. This is called the "blessing bowl." Begin each meal by choosing beads to correspond with things in your life you are grateful for. Create your abundance necklace with beads from this bowl. Make abundance necklaces for others and give them away in spontaneous acts of generosity and prosperity. The more you give, the more you get!

Making Your Abundance Necklace

Tools: chain nose pliers, round nose pliers, scissors, awl

Supplies: beads, charms, Softflex or Beadalon wire, 2x2 crimp tubes, button-style clasp, spacer beads

Steps

A. Make a list of things you are grateful for in your life and the things you want to manifest.

B. Choose beads and charms to represent your blessings, both the old and the new.

C. Cut a wire 2x the length of your necklace plus 4 extra inches for finishing.

D. Begin by making a loop for your button clasp. String enough beads onto the wire to make a loop that will slip over the clasp easily. Then string a bead through both ends of the wire simultaneously, to secure the loop. (fig. 1) This will create a double-strand necklace form with a loop at one end of the necklace. Your button clasp should slip through the loop snugly, so your bracelet won't fall off when finished. (fig. 2)

E. Begin to string beads onto the two wires.

F. When you want to attach charms, you may use the "quick and easy" method or the "wire wrap" method. To string charms the quick and easy way, simply attach them to jump rings with your chain nose pliers, and slip them onto your wire. (fig. 3) Using two jump rings for each charm will keep them more secure. Although the quick and easy method of attaching charms is quick, it is not 100% guaranteed that your charms will stay attached over time. The wire wrap method of securing charms is guaranteed to keep your charms securely in place. However, it does take longer.

G. Follow these steps to wire wrap: Begin by cutting approximately 5 inches of wire. Hold the wire in the middle with chain nose pliers and bend at a 90-degree angle. (fig. 4)

H. Then clamp down on your wire with the round nose pliers in the elbow of the angle. (fig. 5)

I. Wrap the wire around the round nose of the pliers completely until it forms a loop figure that looks like a head with a scarf. (fig. 6)

J. Slip the charm onto the loop. (fig. 7)

K. Now clamp down on the top of the loop with your round nose pliers, while wrapping the "scarf" wire around the "neck" wire with the chain nose pliers. (fig. 8)

L. Stop after rotating the "scarf" wire three times around the "neck" wire. Clip off excess with fingernail clippers. Now your charm will be securely held in the loop. (fig. 9)

M. Next string several beads onto the wire, above the dangling charm. (fig. 10)

N. Repeat the wire wrap procedure again on the remaining end of the wire (steps G-L), leaving this loop empty. This will create a secure loop through which to slip the whole unit onto the wire. (fig. 11)

O. Continue adding beads and charms onto each wire until your necklace is fully strung and ready to be finished.

P. To finish, pass the two strands of wire through a 2x2 crimp tube. (fig. 12)

Q. Then pass both ends of the wires through the wire loop on the back of your button clasp. (fig. 13)

R. Pass the ends of both wires back through the crimp tube and insert the pointy end of the awl into the loop these wires form. (fig. 14) Pull on the ends of the wires with the chain nose pliers while using the awl to create a tight loop with the wire around the clasp. (fig. 15) Slip the awl out when the wire is drawn tightly through the crimp tube, tightly securing the clasp.

S. Clamp down on the crimp tube tightly with the chain nose pliers, securing the clasp to the wire. (fig. 16)

T. Cut the excess wire with fingernail clippers and you are finished.

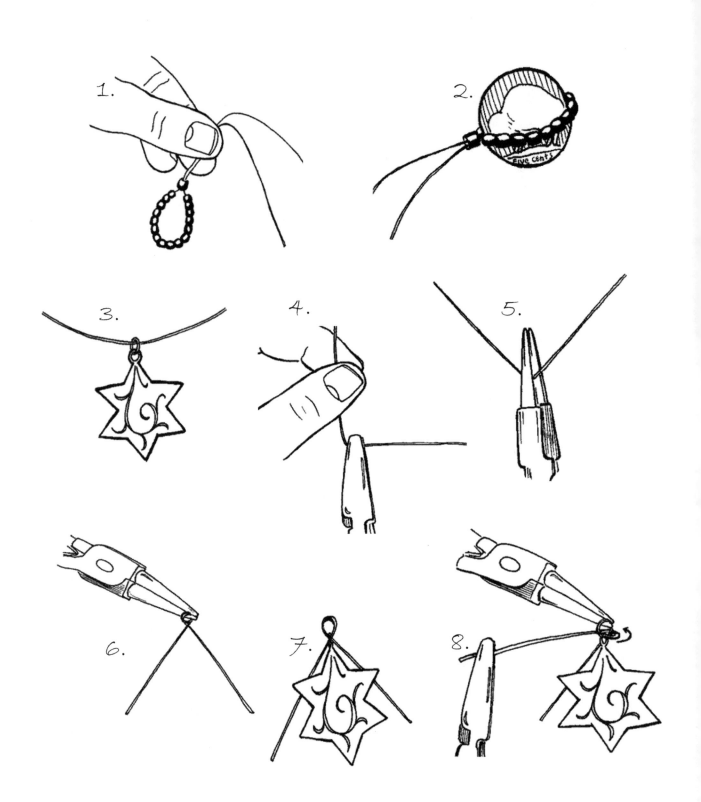

1.

2.

3.

4.

5.

6.

7.

8.

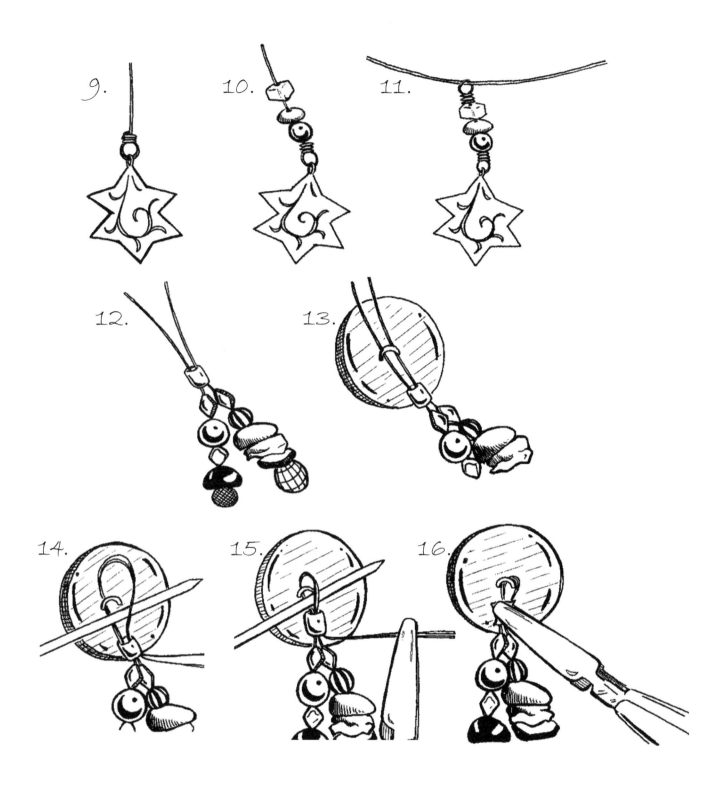

9.

10.

11.

12.

13.

14.

15.

16.

The Dream Catcher and Ritual

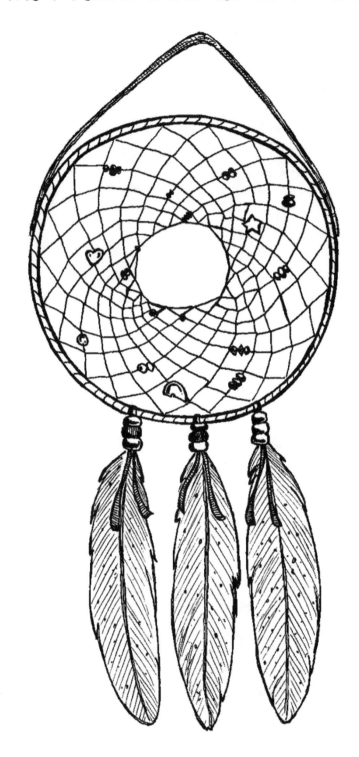

Law #4 of Bead Manifestation:
If You Can SEE It, You Can BEad It, No Matter What It Is
Key word: DREAM
Bead project # 4: The Dream Catcher

Now is the time to make your dream fly. The dream catcher is the power object we will create for this purpose. In the Lakota tradition, dream catchers are used to envision and manifest our dreams. Spider is the spirit of creativity who weaves her web in the world and effortlessly catches her dreams. We will weave beads, charms, colors, and prayers into our webs and embellish them with feathers to make our dreams fly.

Dream Bead Ritual:
Lie down on the floor and get comfortable. Imagine yourself standing on a mountaintop on a warm summer's day. It is ten years from now and the life you are living is all you

dreamed of and more. You look out into the valley below and see your life in front of you. How did you get to the top of the mountain? Turn around and trace your steps back down the path you climbed to the top. What steps did you take? What helpers or guides accompanied you on your journey? What is the source of your power?

When you are done with this visualization exercise, write down what you saw:

Your dream
Your steps up the mountain
Your guides and helpers (these may be animal, spirit, plant, or human)

Then choose seven things from your vision that you would like to manifest in your life and choose seven charms, beads, stone chips, or crystals to represent them. Now it is time to assemble your dream catcher. When you finish your dream catcher, hang it on the wall across from your bed. Go to sleep each night meditating on your vision. Then go out into the world and catch your dreams.
Begin today.

Making Your Dream Catcher

Tools and Materials: metal craft hoop or flexible stick, feathers, 4 pieces of suede 8" length x 1/8" thickness, 1 piece of suede 1/4" thick and long enough to wrap around your metal hoop, feathers, crow beads, favorite beads, stone chips, and charms, artificial sinew, yarn, or dental floss

Steps

A. Begin by choosing charms, beads, and stone chips to symbolize your dreams.

B. Decide if you want to use a metal hoop or flexible stick for your frame. If you are going to use a hoop, wrap the hoop with a 1/4" thick piece of suede. (fig. 1). Start by gluing one end of the suede to the hoop. Make sure it is lying down flatly against the hoop before you begin. Begin to wrap the suede around the hoop, making sure not to overlap the suede as you go along. Stop wrapping when you return to the beginning. Finish off by securing the suede to the hoop with a drop of glue.

C. If you are going to use a stick, you must choose a stick that will allow you to bend it into a circle. When you have the stick bent in a circular form, overlap both ends and wrap them with artificial sinew. (fig. 2) You are ready to begin weaving your web.

D. Tie one end of the artificial sinew (yarn or dental floss) on the hoop or stick. Wrap the sinew around the hoop as shown in the picture, making loops in even intervals. (fig. 3) Make sure you pull the sinew tightly as you go along. The smaller you make the spaces between your loops, the more intricate your web will be. Be sure to add beads, charms, and stone chips as you go along.

E. Stop and tie a square knot when the hole in the center of the dream catcher becomes the size you want. (fig. 4)

F. Attach 1/8" thick pieces of suede lace fringe to the dream catcher by draping them over the bottom of the dream catcher. (fig. 5) Thread crow beads through both ends of the suede and move the beads up until they secure the suede fringe to the bottom of the dream catcher. (fig. 6) Attach a feather to each piece of fringe by putting glue on the end and inserting the base of the feather into the crow bead. (fig. 7)

G. Now tie your 8" x 1/8" lace of suede to the top of the hoop, so that it forms an upside-down V shape, which you will use to hang it. (fig. 8)

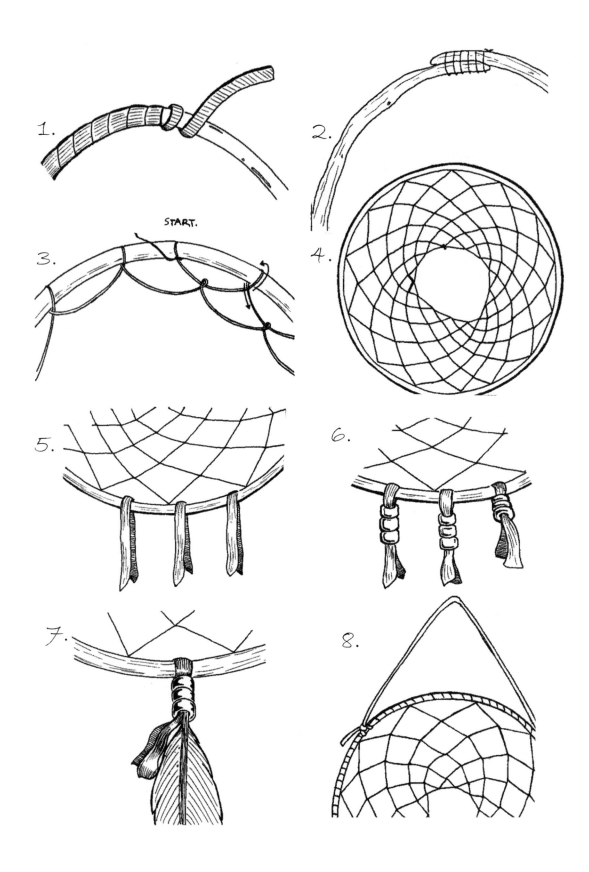

1.

2.

3. START.

4.

5.

6.

7.

8.

The Transformation Rattle and Ritual

Law #5 of Bead Manifestation:
Trust the Invisible Energy That Brings Change
Key words: TRUST CHANGE
Bead project #5: Transformational Rattle

Rattles have been used since ancient times to summon Spirit and bring about change. We don't typically think of beads as making music, but they do. The rhythm of the rattle changes our energy and opens us to new channels of consciousness. The music can also produce altered states of being, conducive to visions and creative visualization. When we experience new levels of energy and perceive the world in a different way, life is full of change.

When you make your rattle, fill it with stone chips and beads that are healing stones. Garnet, turquoise, and amber are favorites of mine. Mix your beads with rice, seashells, and corn for fertility, prosperity, and abundance. Filling rattles with paper prayers and affirmations adds power to their manifestation music.

Transformational Rattle Ritual:

The rattle is also a powerful tool for changing emotion from one state into another. Change is notorious for bringing up fear. I like to use this solitary rattle ritual for transforming fear into love and power.

When you are feeling fear, put on some rhythmic music and begin to dance your fear in the center of your power circle. Give your fear a voice by shaking your rattle as you dance. When you feel your energy beginning to move, pick up a power word and continue to dance this word, shaking your rattle, to give voice to this power. Continue to choose words and continue to dance. When you have danced to several power words, sit down and ask yourself this question: "What does my fear need?"

Answer it by drawing a picture. Your image will be a healing message from your unconscious mind. Choose a bead to remind you of your power to transform your energy from one form into another.

Making Your Rattle

Materials: gourd, seed beads, stone chips, shoe polish or leather dye, permanent markers, a stick for the handle, two pieces of deer hide (6" x 1/8"), one rectangular piece of deer hide (4" x 2"), sandpaper, steel wool, wood-burning tool (optional), beads, charms (optional), feathers (optional)

Steps

A. Sand gourd with sandpaper or steel wool until it's smooth.

B. Draw a circle on the top and the bottom of the gourd that is big enough to allow the stick handle to slide smoothly through the gourd with just a hair extra space.

C. Cut two holes along the circles you have drawn on the top and bottom of the gourd. (fig. 1)

D. Slide the stick through the hole to make sure it fits. (fig. 2)

E. Burn designs into your gourd with a wood-burning tool or draw designs on your gourd with a permanent marker. (fig. 3)

F. Stain the gourd with leather dye or shoe polish, then rub with a soft polishing cloth. If you have used permanent marker, you may want to touch up your images for a brighter look.

G. Fill your gourd with seed beads, garnet, amethyst, and turquoise stone chips. Add paper prayers, words, and dreams. Then insert the stick.

H. Seal the top and bottom of your gourd with glue. (fig. 4) Wrap the top of the stick with a 1/8"x 5" piece of deer hide, where it meets the gourd. (fig. 5) Wrap the stick with a 2"x 3" piece of hide, where it meets the bottom hole of the gourd. (fig. 6) Then wrap this piece of hide with another 1/8"x 5" piece of deer hide or ribbon. (fig. 7)

I. Embellish the handle with beads, charms, and feathers. (fig. 8)

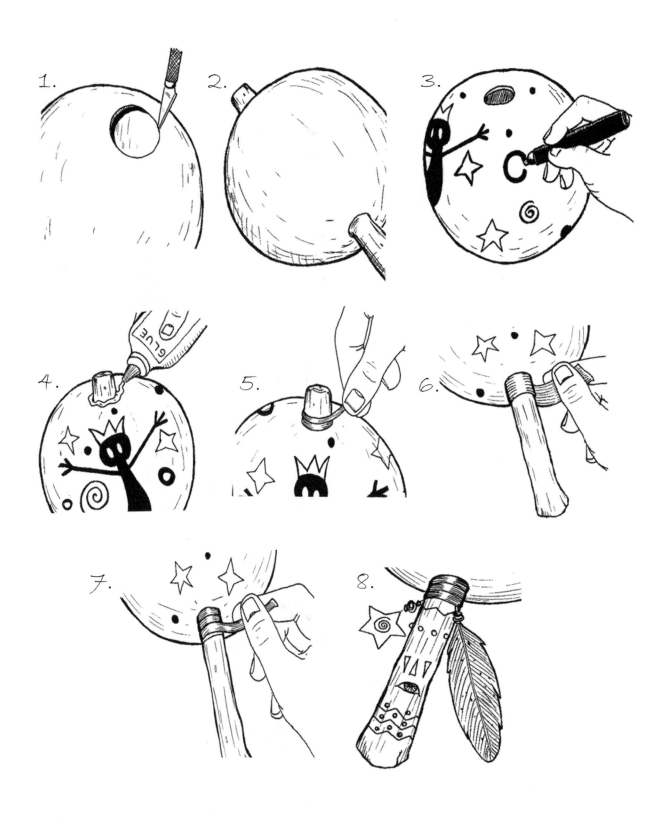

1.

2.

3.

4.

5.

6.

7.

8.

The Spirit Doll and Ritual

Law #6 Of Bead Manifestation:
You Are Full of Grace
Key word: GRACE
Bead project #6: The Spirit Doll

Spirit dolls are powerful medicine. They are magical totems that carry the energy of the Creator, acting as spirit guides, messengers, and protectors. I call mine Grace because Grace is always there when we truly need her. Grace appears when we trust that all is happening for our highest good and open our arms to receive her.

I use my doll Grace in solitary rituals, when what I need is more than I can seem to offer myself. I may need to forgive a loved one, for example, yet all my mind can do is recite a convincing list of reasons why forgiveness is totally out of the question. This is when Grace comes to the rescue.

After you make your doll, you may be surprised by the life energy she exudes. Go ahead and use some of this energy for your own healing and personal transformation. Pin or sew beads and charms on your doll, symbolizing what it is you need to receive. Then trust that help is on your way, even if it doesn't appear in the form you are expecting it.

Spirit Doll Ritual: Spend ritual and meditation time with your Spirit doll. Meditate with Grace in the center of your power circle, and trust that she has connections in powerful places. Begin to surround her with objects that represent your dream. Have Faith in your ability to manifest your vision, whatever it may be!

Making Your Spirit Doll

Materials: For a quick doll body, use a sock stuffed with rags, a rock, or a stick. For embellishment, use beads, charms, acrylic paint, buttons, bottle caps, fabric, glue or glue gun, yarn, tinsel, ribbons, wire, feathers, and whatever you can dream of

Steps

A. Make the body of your doll with a stick or stuffed sock.
B. Create her/his face with beads, paint, and imagination.
C. Embellish the body with prayers, beads, feathers, fabric, charms, etc.
D. Use glue or a glue gun, or a needle and thread, to attach embellishments.
E. Say a prayer while making your doll.
F. Sit with your doll when you are finished and hold her in your arms.

G. Ask her these questions:
   "What is your name?"
   "What is your gift?"
   "What have you come here to do?"
H. Meditate with your doll. When you are
   done, ask yourself these same questions.
   Write it all down and consult your doll
   for guidance and direction.

Law #7 of Bead Manifestation:
You Are a Channel for Healing Energy!
Key word: HEALING
Bead project #7: The Prayer Flag

Healing is what true Art is all about. Prayer flags are bold, colorful, and magical banners celebrating our healing powers. In the artistic process, we channel our vision from a divine source. Our vision shows us in a glimpse, the path of our true destiny. Our healing vision may come in a dream or in a meditation. It may come in symbols, images, or words. Whatever form the messenger takes, it needs to be received, honored, and understood by our hearts and minds together.

We are healed and heal others when we listen to the path of our true destiny and follow this path regardless of our fears. The healing question is "How are we going to spend this lifetime we have been gifted with?" Once we begin to follow our hearts, we oftentimes heal our bodies in the process.

When we live our lives as healing journeys, there will be stones, fences, and sometimes boulders in our paths. We just keep walking forward, knowing that while each step may not feel secure, it certainly feels alive. I showed you my prayer flag. Now I ask you the question "What is your prayer?"

Prayer Flag Ritual: I have a vision of a global art ritual....We will all create prayer flags. They will honor the spirits of all things... animals, art, gun control, children, rivers, world peace, the elderly, diversity, and countless other dreams. This will be a traveling art show, accompanied by music, chanting, and song.

Our intention is planetary healing and transformation of the human spirit. Viewers may participate in a live art experience by creating their own prayer flags and sending prayers together. This ritual can be modified to fit any healing ceremony. I hope someday we will meet in this place.

Making Your Prayer Flag

Materials: fabric, needles, thread, pins, shells, charms, beads, and other embellishments, fabric paint (optional)

Steps

A. Visualize a shape that you find healing.

B. Visualize a color that you find healing. Go to a fabric store or thrift shop and let yourself have a sensual adventure, while choosing the perfect fabric for your flag. Or perhaps you already have this fabric in an old beloved dress or shirt. Old clothes, full of energy and experience, make wonderful prayer flags. Cut your chosen shape out of the piece of fabric that will be your flag.

C. Iron the fabric and turn the edges under.

D. Hem the edges with glue or thread so they won't fray.

E. Begin to paint, sew, or bead your vision onto your flag.

F. Fill your flag with loving kindness. Make each stitch a prayer.

The God Gourd and Ritual

Law #8 of Bead Manifestation:
If It's Not Love, Throw It Away!
Key word: LOVE
Bead project #8: The God Gourd

Gourds have been used as sacred vessels, rattles, and instruments since the earliest times. The God Gourd is a transformational vessel that helps release negative thought and emotion. Simply take unwanted thoughts or feelings, write them on paper, and put them in your God Gourd.

God Gourd Bead Ritual: Burning negative thoughts is my favorite God Gourd ritual. After I fill my God Gourd with paper, I empty it out and light my thoughts on fire. I watch them turn to ashes, then I write down affirmations. I put beads in the God Gourd to plant these new thoughts and to welcome new energy. The next day, I make a necklace with the beads in the God Gourd and I give it away. Love is the gift of the God Gourd.

Making Your Own God Gourd

Tools and Materials: gourd, X-acto knife, plastic tub or sink, leather dye or shoe polish, steel wool, soft cloths, permanent markers, paint, wood-burning tool, beads, waxed linen thread, awl, sandpaper

Steps

A. Wash gourd in soapy, warm water, scrubbing with steel wool to remove dirt or sand down bumps.

B. Dry gourd and sand the body until smooth with sandpaper and steel wool.

C. Draw a line with a pencil around the top of the gourd. (fig. 1)

D. Cut the top off the gourd with an X-acto knife. (fig. 2)

E. Hollow out the gourd and remove all inner matter.

F. Sand the edges around the top of the gourd. (fig. 3)

G. If you are going to decorate the gourd with a wood-burning tool (which I highly suggest), this is the time to do it. Simply plug in the tool and use it like a pencil, drawing your designs on the surface of the gourd. (fig. 4) Then stain and polish your gourd with leather dye or shoe polish.

H. If you don't use a wood-burning tool, you may want to decorate with permanent magic markers before you apply the leather dye or shoe polish.

I. When the gourd is dry, you may embellish it with beads. Simply poke holes in the gourd with your awl, then string beads on the waxed linen and embellish your gourd. (fig. 5)

J. Polish your gourd with a soft cloth.

1.

2.

3.

4.

5.

Gourd Sources

The Paso Robles Pumpkin and Gourd Farm
101 Creston Road
Paso Robles, CA 93446
805-238-0624

Welburn Gourd Farm
Fallbrook, CA 92028
760-728-4271
e-mail: info@welburngourdfarm.com

 Find out more from:
American Gourd Society
P.O. Box 274
Mt. Gilead, OH 53338-0274

"Bead" in many languages

السُّبْحَة
(Arabic)
SŪBHA

মুটি
(Bangla/Bengal)
MŌTI

ΧΑΝΤΡΕΣ
(Greek and Cypriot)
HANDRAYS

موتی
MŌTI
(Urdu)

(Burmese)
KAYUKAMA

חֲרוּזִית
(Hebrew)
HUIYA

ビーズ
(Japanese)
BIZU

manik-manik
(Indonesian)

เม็ด
(Thai)
MED

In Nigeria, the Yoruba say bead "iléké." (i-lay-kay)

In Sierra Leone, the word for bead is "kpoyei" (poy-ay). "Mimi" means small bead.

In France, the word for bead is "perle." In Italy, it's "perla."

In the Wolof tribe of Senegal, the word for bead is "chuka."

The Hausa are the bead traders of West Nigeria and much of West Africa... They call chevron beads "bati moutouk" and millefiori beads "cha cha sou."

In Gambia, the Soninké word for bead is "hanyo."

BEAD SOCIETIES AND MUSEUMS

ALABAMA

Huntsville Bead Society, e-mail: Aclement01@aol.com

ALASKA

Alaska Bead Society, 1231 Gambell St., Anchorage, AK 99501, (907) 269-3444 or (907) 243-4159, e-mail: gv27178@ibm.net

Juneau Bead Society, (907)586-3223, e-mail: beadgal@ptialaska.net

MAT-SU Valley Bead Society, HC01 Box 6454N, Palmer, AK, e-mail: shanigan@mtaonline.net

ARIZONA

Arizona Bead Society, P.O. Box 80111, Arcadia Station 072 (85060-0111), (602)254-2825

CALIFORNIA

The Northern California Bead Society, P.O. Box 12994, Berkeley, CA 94701, (510) 869-2723

Central California Bead Society, Fresno, CA, e-mail: jrfarris@lightspeed.net

The Bead Society of Los Angeles, P.O. Box 241874, Los Angeles, CA 90024-9674, Web site: http://home.att.net/beadsla/

Beadazzled Beaders Society, P.O. Box 51133, Riverside, CA 92517-2133, e-mail: marj.curtis.bd@pe.net

San Diego Bead Society, P.O. Box 230325, San Diego, CA, e-mail: bethrisa@aol.com

The Bead Society of Orange County, 2002 N. Main St., Santa Ana, CA 92706, (714) 828-8468, Web site: http://ftp.oc-net.com/users/udok/beadsoc.htm.

COLORADO

Rocky Mountain Bead Society, P.O. Box 480721, Denver, CO 80248-0721, (303) 271-1676, e-mail: beads@ecentral.com

CONNECTICUT

Connecticut Bead Society, (203)467-6050, e-mail: pnwher@snet.net

FLORIDA

The Bead Society of Central Florida, 121 Larkspur Drive, Altamonte Springs, FL 32701, e-mail: pollym@ao.net

Palm Beach Bead Society, P.O. Box 222, Delray Beach, FL 33447, e-mail: floyd3@bellsouth.net

Bead Society of Gainesville, 4205 NW 16th Blvd., Gainesville, Florida 32605, (352) 379-1272

Tampa Bay Bead Society, P.O. Box 1633, Pinellas Park, FL 33780, e-mail: beadingheart@i.j.net

Treasure Coast Bead Society, P.O. Box 8805, Port St. Lucie, FL 34985, (561) 871- 6144, e-mail: snooch101@aol.com

Florida West Coast Bead Society, P.O. Box 1074, Sarasota, FL 34234-1074, (941) 925-3403

The Bead Society of North Florida, 2050 N. Monroe St., Tallahassee, FL 32303, (850) 383-1776, e-mail: beadh20@tallynet.com

GEORGIA

Atlanta Bead Society, PMB #142, Suite 203, 4651 Woostock Rd., Roswell, GA 30075-1686, (770) 928-5726; e-mail: weebluboat@aol.com

Southern Flames, Society of Glass Beadmakers, Atlanta Chapter, 3048 W. Roxboro Rd., Atlanta, GA 30355, (404)264-9358; e-mail: southern-flames@mindspring.com

HAWAII

Bead Society of Hawaii, Oahu Chapter, P.O. Box 235578, Oahu, HI 96823-3509, e-mail: dottie2lava.net

IDAHO

Coeur d'Alene Bead Society, 3311N. 15th St., Coeur d'Alene, ID 83815, (208)664-9552, e-mail: zizzy@micron.net

ILLINOIS

Chicago Midwest Bead Society, Ayla Phillips, c/o Ayla's Originals, 1511 Sherman Ave., Chicago, Il 960201, (847) 328-4040, e-mail: ayla@Ayla'soriginals.com

Bead Society of Greater Chicago, P.O. Box 8103, Chicago, Il 960091-8103, (312) 458-0519

KENTUCKY

Bowling Green Beaders Guild, c/o 753 Park Street, Bowling Green, KY 42101, (270)842-2636

LOUISIANA

Baton Rouge Bead Society, 919 Bromley Drive, Baton Rouge, LA 70808, (225) 767-3094, Web site: www.br-beads.com

New Orleans Bead Society, 114 Midway Drive, River Ridge, LA 70123, (504) 737-2986

MARYLAND

The Baltimore Bead Society, Louella Duncan, P.O. Box 311, Riderwood, MD 21139, (410) 882-4120

The Bead Society of Greater Washington, P.O. Box 70036, Chevy Chase, MD 20813-0036, (301) 277-6830; e-mail: bsgw@erols.com; Web site: www.bsgw.org

MASSACHUSETTS

Beadesigner International, The Bead Society of New England, Gudrun Wolpow, membership, 135 Aspinwall Ave., Brookline, MA 02446, (508) 785-9097, e-mail: milliefiori@aol.com, website: www.geocities.com\soho\3542

MICHIGAN

Great Lakes Beadworkers' Guild, P.O. Box 1639, Royal Oak, MI 48068, (810) 997-7043

MINNESOTA

Upper Midwest Bead Society, St. Paul, MN, Sandy Graves, (651) 645-0304

MISSOURI

St. Louis Bead Society, e-mail: sbuskirk@gems-beads.com

NEBRASKA

Nebraska Bead Society, 3419 J Street, Lincoln, NE 68510, (402) 484-7545; e-mail: april@canoe.unl.edu

NEVADA

The Las Vegas Bead Society, (707) 656-1144, e-mail: skibeads@ix.net-com.com

NEW JERSEY

Bead Society of New Jersey, P.O. Box 537, Colts Neck, NJ 07722, (732) 521-2971, e-mail: SuzanneHye@aol.com

South Jersey Bead Society, P.O. Box 5321, Delanco, NJ 08075, e-mail: SJBS99@aol.com

NEW MEXICO

New Mexico Bead Society, 4201 San Pedro NE #221, Albuquerque, NM 87109-2034, (505) 884-5433

NEW YORK

New York Polymer Clay Guild, P.O. Box 786, Murray Hill Station, NY 10156, (718) 499-8728, e-mail: tempestal@aol.com

Bead Society of Greater New York, P.O. Box 427, NY, NY 10116-0427, (212) 496-6966

NORTH CAROLINA

Triangle Bead Society, Sally Lewis c/o Bead Struk, 715 W. Johnson, Suite 104, Raleigh, NC 27603, (919) 833-6070, e-mail: beadstruk@aol.com

OKLAHOMA

Oklahoma Bead Society, Joyce Sandifer, RR1, Box 3480, Adair, OK 74137, e-mail: tetonnana1@aol.com

OREGON

Portland Bead Society, P.O. Box 10611, Portland, OR 97296, (503) 691-2126, e-mail: beadport@hevanet.com; Web site: www.hevanet.com/bead-port

PENNSYLVANIA

Brandywine Bead Society, 1840 Tall Oaks Road, Orwigsburg, PA 17961, (570) 366-2300, e-mail: brandybead@voicenet.com

TEXAS

Austin Bead Society, P.O. Box 656, Austin, TX 78767-0656, e-mail: pamlarson@juno.com; Web site: www.austinbeadsociety.org

Southeast Texas Bead and Ornament Society, 13560 Inwood Drive, Beaumont, TX 77713, (409) 753-2950; Web site: www.Virtualhosts.net/setbos

Bay Area Bead Society, 4314 Peridot Ln., Friendswood, TX 77546, (281) 474-2003; e-mail: beadconnec@aol.com

Houston Bead Society, 2409 Perthius Dr., Houston, TX 77568, (409) 938-0393

San Antonio Bead and Ornament Society, P.O. Box 700611, San Antonio, TX 78270-0611; e-mail: cherinewman@yahoo.com

VIRGINIA

The Northern Virginia Bead Society, P.O. Box 2465, Fairfax, VA 22031, (703) 273-2493

The Bead Society of Southeastern Virginia, 801 Marlbank Dr., Yorktown, VA 23692, (757) 890-0547; e-mail: cchenoweth@dollartree.com

WASHINGTON

Northwest Bead Society, 810 3rd Ave., Suite 140-41, Seattle, WA 98104, (425) 485-6673; e-mail: rddesign@rddesigns.com; Web site: www.rddesigns.com/nwbs.htm

Spokane-Northwest Bead Society, P.O. Box 40225, Spokane, WA 99202, (509) 926-5758

WASHINGTON, D.C.

The Bead Society of Greater Washington, P.O. Box 70036, Chevy Chase, MD 20813-0036, (301) 277-6830; e-mail: bsgw@erols.com; Web site: www.bsgw.org

WISCONSIN

Madison Bead Society, P.O. Box 260415, Madison, WI 53726-0415, (608) 242-9282, e-mail: gloder@wha.org

CANADA

Toronto Bead Society, Pat Rogal, (416) 921-8534

GREAT BRITAIN

The Bead Society of Great Britain, 1 Casburn Ln., Burwell, Cambridge, England CB5 0ED;44 1638742024; e-mail: carole@morrises.keme.co.uk; Web site: http://membersdelphi.com/britishbeads/index.html

OTHER SOURCES OF INFORMATION

The Bead Directory

by Linda Benmour. Ben-Stone Press, P.O. Box 10103, Dept. 0196, Oakland, CA 94610; (510) 452-0836. The Bead Directory is a comprehensive directory of available sources of beads and bead supplies. The Bead Directory also contains full descriptions of bead societies, a bead bazaar calendar, listings of magazines, museums, and classes.

The Complete Bead Resource Book

By Patricia Abahusayn. Sandburg Publishing, 4432 Sandburg Way, Irvine, CA 92612; fax: (949) 786-7081; e-mail: Beadgirl2@aol.com . The 4th edition contains over 2,500 resources for beads, including bead artists, bead shows, publications, and associations. It is regularly updated.

Bead Museums

The Bead Museum, 5754 W. Glenn Dr., Glendale, AZ 85301; phone/fax (623) 930-7395; Web site: www.TheBeadMuseum.com

Bead Museum in D.C. and BSGW Learning Center, 400 7th St. NW, Washington, D.C. 20004, (202) 624-4500, e-mail: beadmus@erols.com; Web site: www.thebeadmuseum.org

The Picard Trade Bead Museum, 27885 Berwick Drive, Carmel, CA 93923; (831) 624-4138, e-mail: info@picardbeads.com

BIBLIOGRAPHY

Jamey D. Allen, EYE BEADS AND MAGIC AMULETS (1996 Calendar)

Angeles Arrien, SIGNS OF LIFE: THE FIVE UNIVERSAL SHAPES AND HOW TO USE THEM, Jeremy P. Tarcher/ Putnam, NY, NY (1998)

Nancy Blair, AMULETS OF THE GODDESS, ORACLE OF ANCIENT WISDOM, Wingbow Press, Oakland, CA (1993)

Lapidary Journal, THE BEAD ANNUAL, Bead Roll Call (October 2000)

Lois Sherr Dubin, THE HISTORY OF BEADS, Harry N. Abrams Inc., NY, NY (1987)

Lois Sherr Dubin, NORTH AMERICAN INDIAN JEWELRY AND ADORNMENT, Harry N. Abrams Inc., NY, NY (1999)

Joan Mowatt Erikson, THE UNIVERSAL BEAD, W.W. Norton & Co., Inc., NY, NY (1993)

Clarissa Pinkola Estés, WOMEN WHO RUN WITH THE WOLVES, Ballantine Books, NY, NY (1992)

Susanne E. Fincher, CREATING MANDALAS: FOR INSIGHT, HEALING, AND SELF-EXPRESSION, Shambhala, Boston, MA (1991)

Angela Fisher, AFRICA ADORNED, Harry N. Abrams, Inc., NY, NY (1984)

Robert K. Liu, COLLECTIBLE BEADS, Ornament, Inc., Vista, CA (1995)

Tim McCreight, THE COMPLETE METALSMITH, Davis Publications, (1991)

Melody, LOVE IS IN THE EARTH: A KALEIDOSCOPE OF CRYSTALS, Earth Love Publishing House, Wheat Ridge, CO (1995)

Desmond Morris, BODY GUARDS, Element, Boston, MA (1999)

Michael Samuels, M.D., CREATIVE HEALING: HOW TO HEAL YOURSELF BY TAPPING YOUR HIDDEN CREATIVITY, HarperSanFrancisco, NY, NY (1998)

ACKNOWLEDGMENTS

With much gratitude to all those who
accompanied me on the journey of this book...
Fritz Fuller; Janie Balesteri, computer goddess;
Joe Leone, extraordinary technical and bead
illustrator; Ling Lucas; Patty Gift; Carrie Thornton;
Kathy "Eagle Mother" Leone, the folks at the Bead
Museum in Glendale, Arizona; Ruth and John Picard
at the Bead Museum in Carmel Valley, California;
Judy Butzine; Abdul and Abraham Touray; Cecily Karle;
The Optimum Health Institute; Lilik Gondopriono; Gao Jie;
Shihoko Nagai, calligraphy queen; Lin Haley, right-hand
muse; William Passero, left-hand muse; Terre Passero;
Mary Troupe; Emily Owen; Susan Pacitto; all the wild
women who have hosted my bead parties over the years;
and my Spirit World Support Staff.
Thank you.

A FINAL WORD...

When you are done creating your own beaded treasures, you will want to sit and listen to what they have to say. The beads tell many stories. Bead tags are the perfect place to write them down. Here's my tag from my very first bead business: "Cal & Al's Bead Trip"

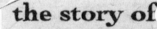

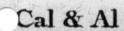

Beader's Creed, according to Cal & Al

Cal and Al believe in unity and love between all peoples brought on by creative intercultural bonding thru beading with BROTHERS & SISTERS of all races, planetary origins & creeds. BEADING HEALS THE PAST SO THAT WE MAY LIVE CREATIVELY AND WITHOUT FEAR IN THE PRESENT. Brought up by wolves in a world that puts a price tag on fur coats, CAL & AL understand loneliness and pain.

"All that exists is the power of love in this present moment, CAL & AL say BEAD IT and so shall you SEE IT." CAL & AL are older than you, and they know. BEADING SAVES LIVES. P.S. Did we tell you, you look BEAUTIFUL in these beads?

B E A D S !

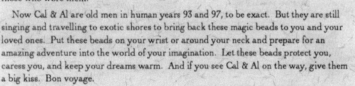

the story of Cal & Al

Cal & Al, sons of a Tuscan Princess and a Bedouin bead trader, were orphaned at a tender age and raised by wolves in honey colored wheat fields south of Shanghai. With no books or toys to fill their hours, the young boys busied themselves stringing beads left to them by their father and singing love songs taught to them by their mother. If only they would bead and sing, their mother promised, their hearts would always be full of wonder and their minds blessed with the many adventures of imagination.

And so it was. In fields of mother's music, Cal & Al strung beads of crimson and gold, journeying to cities, villages, and far away planets. Together they collected magnificent beads of color and light, beads that could heal the darkest wounds of all those who wore them.

Now Cal & Al are old men in human years 93 and 97, to be exact. But they are still singing and travelling to exotic shores to bring back these magic beads to you and your loved ones. Put these beads on your wrist or around your neck and prepare for an amazing adventure into the world of your imagination. Let these beads protect you, caress you, and keep your dreams warm. And if you see Cal & Al on the way, give them a big kiss. Bon voyage.

These are several of my tags from my current bead business: "The Prayer Party"

...harm on ...odern day talisman to activate your personal power. This charm invokes love and divine protection. You are invited to a party to celebrate you! The Prayer Party™ is dedicated to celebrating individual self-expression and creativity through art, spirituality, and community. Bless your heart! Check out our workshops, books, and magical art at....... www.prayerparty.com

Courage

Love
XOX

Creativity

Abundance

This prayer bracelet is to celebrate YOU!
♡
Dare to IMAGINE!
☯
Focus your THOUGHTS!
Make room * for MIRACLES!
☆ BELIEVE!

Limitless
Oneness
Visionary
Energy!

Peace

Creating tags for your own beaded-treasures adds Magic & meaning to your work. It's Your turn now... I can't wait to hear your stories.... ♡

DREAMS

For information on workshops, jewelry,
and other products, please contact
carolyn@prayerparty.com
and visit our website at
www.prayerparty.com

We'll see you there!